Fast Flying Geese

...and more!

Karin Hellaby

Quilters Haven

Publications

Acknowledgements

I had decided that 2004 was to be my year off from writing. I felt I deserved a rest, having written three books in as many years. No sooner had I made the decision than I met a wonderful man. B has become a great companion on travels around the world, and this book is dedicated to him. When I saw geese designs as far afield as the north of Norway, Venice, Geneva, America and Marrakesh I was inspired to start writing again!

Many of you know that I have three sons, and one of the driving forces behind my writing was the need to give them financial support through their university education. Ross has now finished his four-year Economics course, and Jason has begun studying Physics at York. Alexander, the youngest, is still at school, and is worried that there won't be a book for him. Here it is Alexander – a book for you. One that will help you fly the nest!

If I even mention that I am writing a new book then the students who attend classes in my shop, Quilters Haven, will volunteer their help. It is this wonderful group who manage to take my techniques and designs and make them into quilts in three months, as well as putting forward many ideas of their own. This time the offers of help flew in from as far afield as North Carolina, USA and Calgary, Canada. It just goes to show that geese fly all over the world!

Some of the fabric for the quilts was given to us by UK distributors Makower and Oakcraft, as well as Benartex in the US. This has helped to keep the projects up-to-date with the latest gorgeous fabrics in the quilting market.

My usual team have worked their magic on the book – Rosemary Muntus has again excelled herself with the clear, computer-drawn diagrams and Allan Scott, my editor and layout artist, keeps the pair of us co-ordinated. This time we have had the help of a local photographer, Colin Shaw, who has helped to bring the latest digital technology into this aspect of the book.

Finally a big 'thank you' to my readers, who frequently tell me how much they appreciate my books and make all the hard work worthwhile!

Karin Hellaby

Fast Flying Geese Quilts

...and more!
Karin Hellaby

Page 1: Kite Tails *by Heather Langdon*

Page 3: Flower Flight 2 *by Pam Bailey, machine quilted by Jan Chandler*

Left: Spiral in the Sky *by Jan Allen*

First published by
Quilters Haven Publications in 2005

Copyright © Karin Hellaby 2005

Graphics by Rosemary Muntus
Layout by Allan Scott

Photography by Shawphoto,
Tel: +44(0)1394 387328

Printed by Borcombe SP
Premier Way, Abbey Park Industrial Estate,
Romsey, Hampshire SO51 9AQ

ISBN 0-9540928-3-X UPC 7- 44674- 81512-5
Quilters Haven Publications
68 High Street, Wickham Market
Suffolk IP13 0QU, UK

Tel: +44 (0)1728 746275
Fax: +44 (0)1728 746314

www.quilters-haven.co.uk

Contents

Geese basics

The next few pages are important to read, as they cover the basics that will help you with the techniques in this book.

If you are a complete beginner then it really is worth starting at the beginning – the techniques become progressively more difficult as you work through the book. If you are already an experienced patchworker then dip in anywhere that takes your fancy!

High flying geese quilts are all based on a simple block that can be created and used in different ways. This basic block is a rectangle. It is made up of the goose, a large triangle, and the sky (the background fabric) — two triangles on either side of the goose which help to give a finished rectangular unit.

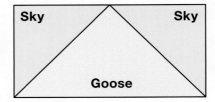

- **Cutting charts**
  On the cutting charts, 'final size' refers to the goose unit width, including the sky.

Final size	Width	Height
4″	4″	2″
6″	6″	3″
8″	8″	4″

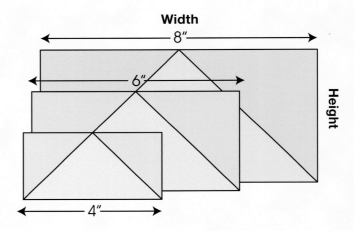

- **Fabrics**
  I recommend you use 100% cotton dress weight fabric for the projects in this book. Your local quilting shop will be able to help you choose your fabric.

- **Cutting strips**
  When you need a strip of fabric, cut it from selvedge to selvedge. Normally the fabric width is approximately 40–42″.

- **Seam allowances**
  A ¼″ seam allowance is used throughout this book. When machine piecing, use a special patchwork foot to give you the correct allowance without the need to mark the fabric.

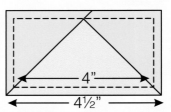

A seamed goose has a ¼″ seam allowance included

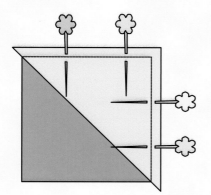

- **Pinning**
  When I have to pin fabrics, I pin at right angles to the seam I am going to sew using a thin flower pin. This holds the fabric together well – and if you forget to remove the pin, your machine needle can move slowly over it without damage.

- **Sewing**
  Sew straight stitches with a slightly smaller than medium stitch: no tying off is needed unless indicated. The stitching should be small enough not to come undone, but large enough to 'unpick' if you go wrong.

- **Pressing seams**
  Unless the instructions state otherwise, press seams in one direction, not open. Seams are normally pressed towards the darker fabric.

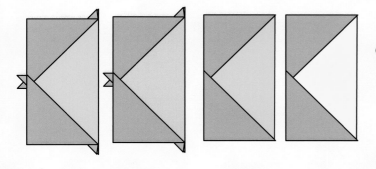

- **Trimming the 'ears'**
  When you join triangles, you often get little 'ears' of fabric that stick out of the block. You can see them clearly in the diagram above. The tidy quilter trims these away after pressing.

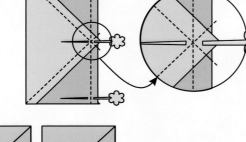

- **Sewing goose units together using X factor**
  Make several geese units and then stitch together into a strip or block. Place pairs of geese right side up, flip one unit over so pairs are right sides together. Stitch using X centre as guideline for correct seam allowance.

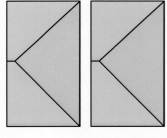

- **Sewing 3D goose units together using clipped seam alignment**
  When you need to stitch two geese together to make a pair, start by laying them right sides up and then flipping one goose over the other, right sides together. Sew from the side of the clipped goose tip using the clipped seam as a guide for your seam line. This will help you retain a tip on your goose when the units are sewn together.

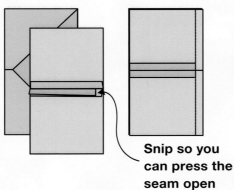

Snip so you can press the seam open

7

● Using up 'waste' triangles

To use up waste fabric triangles (created using my favourite goose technique) sew a second seam ½" away from the original sewing line. Cut between the stitching lines. You will then get an extra half square triangle which you could use for a future project or maybe a border.

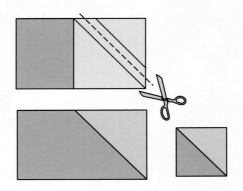

● Creating strip sets

Strip sets are several strips of fabric stitched together along their length. If you are using more than two strips, alternate sewing directions to prevent stretching.

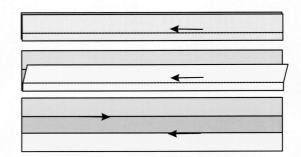

● Pressing finished units

After sewing geese units together you will need to press well in one direction. I usually press away from the goose tip because the fabric easily presses in that direction. However, if you wish to see the X at the geese sides for sewing onto borders then you will need to press in the opposite direction.

● Fussy cutting

If you are using feature fabric you may wish to 'fussy cut'. Place a square ruler on the fabric and move around until you feel you have a good 'picture' underneath.

Check that you have the sides of the square on the fabric grain-lines, i.e. parallel or at right angles to the selvedge. Cut out the square. Move to a different part of the fabric and repeat. You will find that the fabric is full of square holes!

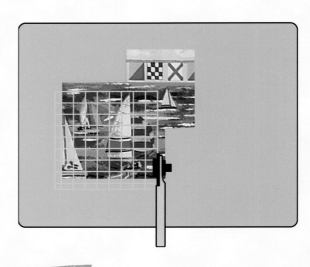

● Fussy appliqué

If you are using feature fabric to create appliqué embellishments, cut out a square larger than the selected item and use fused bonding ironed on to the wrong side of the fabric. Cut out the motifs you require, peel away the protective paper layer, and bond following the manufacturer's instructions.

Creating circle inserts

Setting a circle of geese into a background fabric using this method allows you to 'fudge' to keep those lovely edge points on your geese. The patchwork seam allowances lie flat and this method does not require any 'easing in' of fabrics. Best of all – it's easy!

1 Trace the finished size of circle onto freezer paper. Cut out allowing at least 1" extra around the shape.

2 Press the glossy side of the freezer paper on to the wrong side of the background fabric.

3 Set your sewing machine to a very small straight stitch. Sew on the marked circle line.

4 Draw a ¼" circle inside the stitches. Use this line as your cutting line to remove the inside of the circle (fabric and paper) and leave a ¼" seam allowance. Gently remove the remaining freezer paper from the background fabric.

5 Clip the seam allowance almost to the stitched line, clipping about every ¼"–½" all the way around.

6 Carefully press under the seam allowance so the stitched line does not show on the right side. Remember to maintain the curve.

7 Place on top of patchwork to be inserted. Align and pin or baste into place. Hem down by hand with an invisible stitch or stitch around the circle with an invisible appliqué machine stitch.

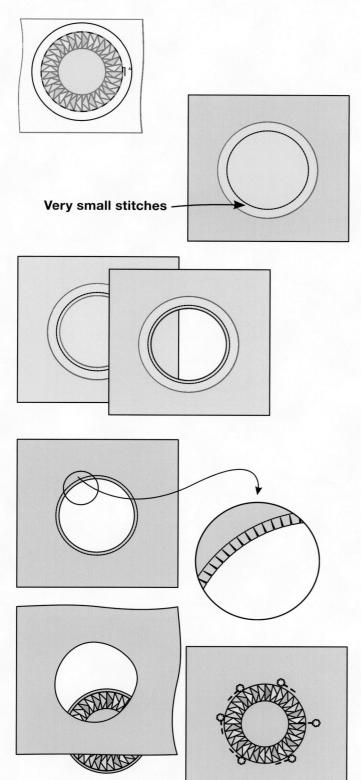

Very small stitches

Speed cutting with rotary cutters

Many of the geese techniques need accurately cut rectangles, squares and triangles. Rotary cutting makes this easy, especially when you need lots of pieces exactly the same size. You will need a rotary cutter, a mat and a ruler. They all come in different sizes, so experiment to find the combination that suits you best. Practice cutting scrap material to gain confidence – and remember, it is easier to cut through three or four layers of fabric than a single layer. The cutter is very sharp, so *always* put the guard back after using it. You must be able to slide the ruler easily over the fabric, and position it correctly; but once you are ready to cut, the ruler must not slide. For this reason I prefer to use the new Omnigrip rulers, or to place some Invisigrip under any ruler that tends to slip.

To cut strips of fabric

1 Iron the fabric. Fold fabric in half, selvedges together, with a good, strong crease along the fold. If you have no selvedges, iron with the fold along the straight of the grain.

2 Place fabric on unmarked side of rotary cutting mat, folded edge nearest you. Lay ruler on top, matching a horizontal line of the ruler to the fabric fold. Use your left hand to hold the ruler in place.

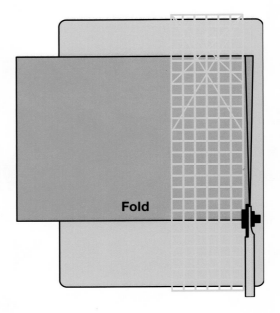

Fold

3 Rotary cut against the right side of the ruler (left handers rotary cut on the left). Remove safety cover on the cutter and lean the cutter against the ruler; hold it firmly, pushing it down with your index finger. Start cutting before crossing the bottom fold, pushing away from you. Always cut away from you, and when you complete the cut, replace the safety guard. This first cut straightens the edge of the fabric.

4 Turn the mat through 180º, or walk to the opposite side of the board. The straight edge you have cut will now be on your left.

5 You are now ready to cut fabric strips. Place the ruler so the exact width measurement you need is precisely aligned to the newly cut edge of the fabric, ensuring the fold is still lined up with one of the horizontal guidelines. Rotary cut as before.

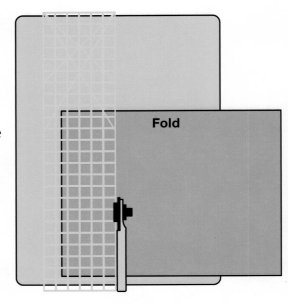

Fold

Multiple squares

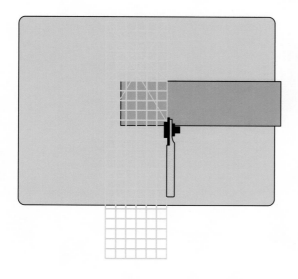

Using 4½″ squares as an example:

1 Place a pre-cut 4½″ fabric strip on the mat. This will be cut while still folded.

2 Square up the strip selvedge end, removing the selvedge completely.

3 Turn the mat through 180º.

4 Lay the ruler on the fabric so that the 4½″ mark lines up with the newly cut edge, and the top of the fabric is in line with a ruler line. Rotary cut. Each cut will give you two squares.

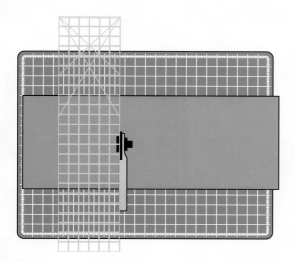

For strips and squares larger than the width of your ruler:

1 Use the printed side of the mat; line up the cut edge of the fabric against the 0 line down the side of the mat.

2 Position the strip so that it runs along the parallel lines of the mat; place the ruler on the correct vertical line and cut.

Cutting one square

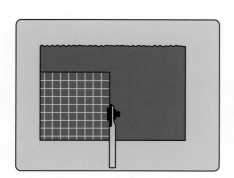

Using an 8″ square as an example:

1 Place the 8½″ square ruler in the bottom left-hand corner of the fabric. Trim away excess fabric on the right and top edges.

2 Remove the ruler, and rotate the fabric square through 180º.

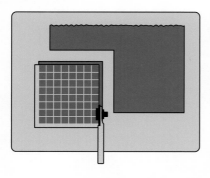

3 Place the 8″ lines of the ruler on the newly cut edges.

4 Cut the remaining two sides of your square to the right and along the top of the repositioned ruler.

11

Finishing

Layering and quilting

Layer your quilt top with wadding and backing. Safety pin together or baste.

Hand or machine quilt as desired.

Trim off excess backing and wadding.

Binding

Join together 2¼" wide fabric strips, until you have a strip long enough to go completely round the quilt with 10" extra.

1 Cut the beginning of the binding at a 45-degree angle. Turn in edge ¼" and press.

2 Fold the binding strip in half lengthways, wrong sides together, and press.

3 Place the binding on the right side of the quilt, aligning raw edges of the binding and the quilt. My starting point is on the bottom quilt edge, about 6" away from a corner.

4 Using a walking foot, begin sewing 2" from the strip end, and, stopping ¼" from the first quilt corner, backstitch.

5 Remove the quilt from the machine and cut the threads.

6 Fold the binding up, then back down so that the fold is even with the quilt edge. Pin.

7 Begin stitching at the edge of the next side, backstitching to secure the threads. Continue sewing to the next corner. Repeat at all four corners.

8 As you near the start point, cut the binding strip and tuck the end inside the folded strip. Finish the sewing and backstitch.

9 Turn binding to back of quilt, and blindstitch to backing. Fold corners as shown.

And finally...

Label your quilt with your name and date.

Sit back and admire your hard work!

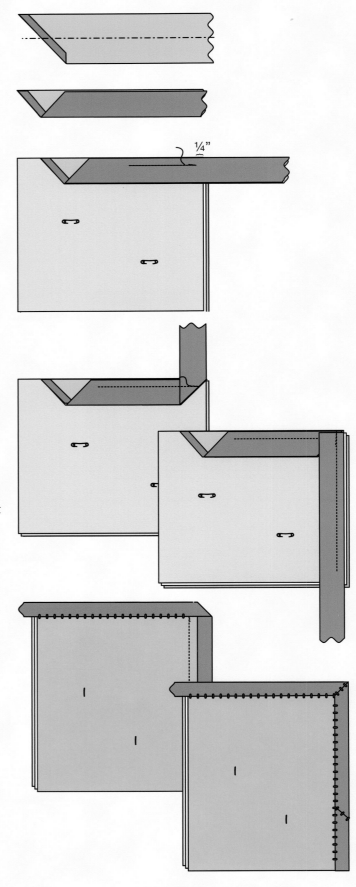

Introducing a few of the fascinating techniques in this
book – find out more on the following pages!

Traditional geese

Traditionally, the Flying Geese patchwork unit is made from three triangles sewn together into a rectangle. The centre goose triangle has one sky triangle on either side. There is no waste fabric with this method but you will have to stitch along two bias seams, which can stretch. You may wish to spray starch your fabric to make it crisp and therefore less likely to stretch. This technique is ideal for hand as well as machine sewing..

Easy cutting chart

Final width	Sky sq (4)	Goose sq (1 makes 4 geese)
4"	2⅞"	5¼"
6"	3⅞"	7¼"
8"	4⅞"	9¼"

1 Cut the sky square into two triangles by making one diagonal cut.

2 Cut the goose square into four triangles by cutting from corner to corner diagonally.

3 Stitch the triangles together. Place all three triangles (two sky and one goose) right sides up in rectangle formation. Flip one sky triangle right sides down on goose, matching base line raw edges. Stitch with ¼" seam allowance. Press away from goose. Repeat with other sky triangle and press again away from goose. Cut off fabric 'ears'.

4 Make several geese units and then stitch together into a strip or block.

My Alberta Home
by Anne Dale and Kathy Holt, Calgary, Canada (57" × 72")

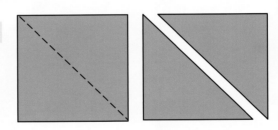

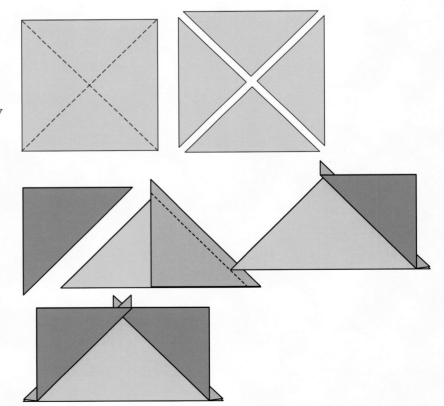

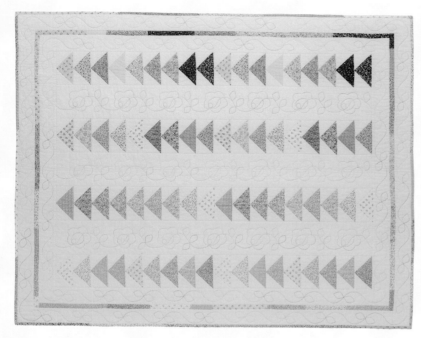

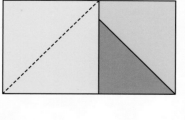

Flower Flight *by Pam Bailey (54" × 64")*

This method avoids having to sew those nasty bias seams. There is some fabric waste, but as there is less 'stretch' you may be happier with the goose! Take a look at Geese basics on page 8 if you would like an idea to help you use up any waste fabric.

Easy cutting chart

Final width	Sky sq (2)	Goose (1)
4"	2½"	2½" × 4½"
6"	3½"	3½" × 6½"
8"	4½"	4½" × 8½"

1 Mark sky squares on the wrong side with a diagonal line.

2 Place one sky square right side down on goose rectangle matching corners. Stitch on marked diagonal line. Remove excess fabric leaving a ¼" seam. Press sky away from goose. Trim away 'ear'.

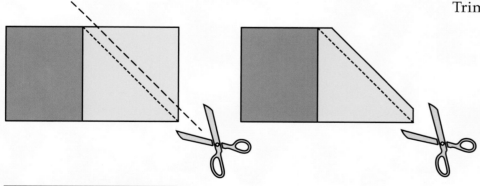

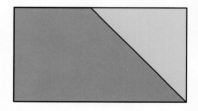

3 Repeat with second sky fabric in opposite corner of goose.

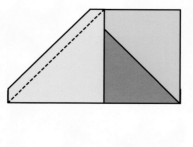

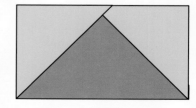

Nosy geese

Detail from I Love Cats *by Julia Reed*

Nosy geese have triangle tips in a colour that contrasts with the main goose unit. By choosing your fabric carefully you can decide if you want the nose to dominate or not.

Easy cutting chart

Final width	Sky sq (cut two)	Goose*
4″	2½″	1½″ × 4½″
6″	3½″	2″ × 6½″
8″	4½″	2½″ × 8½″

*cut two rectangles, one from each of two contrasting fabrics

1 Stitch the two goose rectangles right sides together, sewing along the longer side.

Depending on the finished size you now have either:
- a 2½″ × 4½″ rectangle (4″)
- a 3½″ × 6½″ rectangle (6″)
- or a 4½″ × 8½″ rectangle (8″)

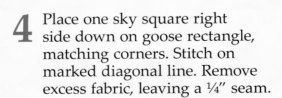

2 Press the seam open.

3 Mark sky squares on the wrong side with a diagonal line.

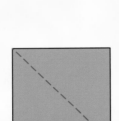

4 Place one sky square right side down on goose rectangle, matching corners. Stitch on marked diagonal line. Remove excess fabric, leaving a ¼″ seam.

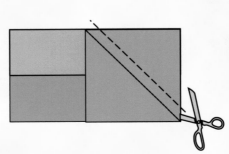
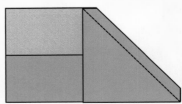

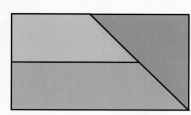

5 Press sky away from goose.

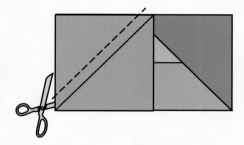

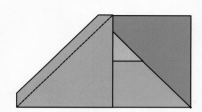

6 Repeat with second sky fabric in opposite corner of goose.

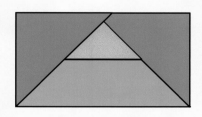

What if...

...you varied the width of the 'nose' fabric ?

...the sky and 'nose' fabrics were the same?

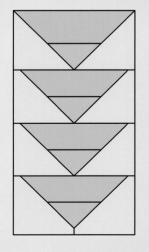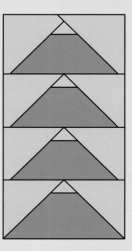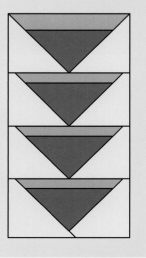

Racing geese

This goose variation uses a centre contrast fabric strip. It looks as if the geese are racing around a quilt border!

Easy cutting chart

Final width	Sky sq (2)	Goose centre	Goose sides (2)
4″	2½″	2″ × 2½″	1¾″ × 2½″
6″	3½″	2″ × 3½″	2¾″ × 3½″
8″	4½″	2½″ × 4½″	3½″ × 4½″

Racing Geese in the East *by Tricia Thornton (29″ square)*

1 Make a rectangle with the three geese rectangles by placing the single colour in the centre and the two remaining rectangles one on each side on either side.

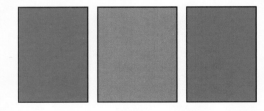

2 Stitch right sides together, sewing along the longer sides. Press open. Depending on the finished size you now have either:
- a 2½″ × 4½″ rectangle (4″)
- a 3½″ × 6½″ rectangle (6″)
- or a 4½″ × 8½″ rectangle (8″)

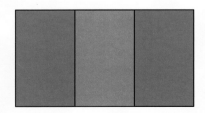

3 Mark sky squares on the wrong side with a diagonal line.

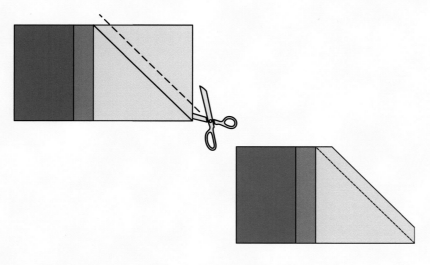

4 Place one sky square right side down on goose rectangle matching corners. Stitch on marked diagonal line. Remove excess fabric leaving a ¼″ seam. Press sky away from goose.

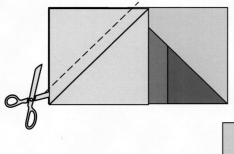

5 Repeat with the second sky square in the opposite corner of the goose.

Multiple geese

Cut three strips of fabric.

Final size	Centre strip	Side strips (2)
4″	2″	1¾″
6″	2″	2¾″
8″	2½″	3½″

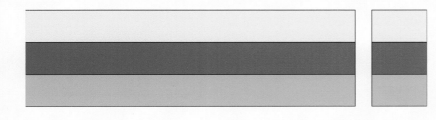

Stitch fabric strips together along the length to make a strip set. Press seams open. Cut geese rectangles, e.g. 42″ will cut into sixteen 4″ geese.

Make a whole flock of geese by strip piecing the central strip to the two side strips and then cutting the goose rectangles.

What if...

...each goose side was a different fabric?

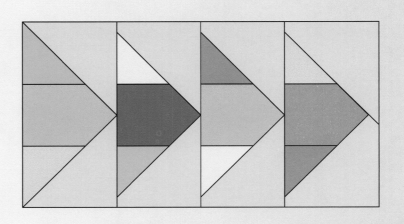

Diamond geese

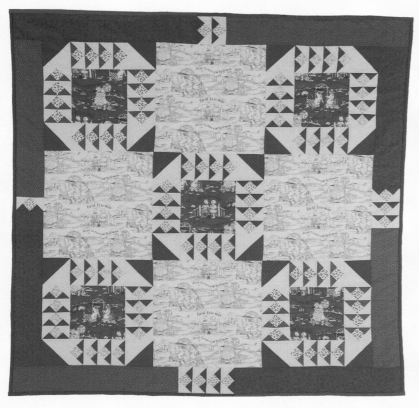

A diamond shape becomes the goose tip in this intriguing variation. All you have to do is to make a goose unit and then add sky triangles.

Easy cutting chart

Final width	Sky sq (2)	Goose diamond	Goose triangles sq (2)
4″	2½″	2″ × 4½″	2½″
6″	3½″	3½″ × 6½″	3½″
8″	4½″	4½″ × 8½″	4½″

Best Friends *by*
Dena Daniels
(56″ square)

1 Mark goose triangle squares on the wrong side with a diagonal line.

2 Place one right side down on goose rectangle, matching corners. Stitch on marked diagonal line. Remove excess fabric leaving a ¼″ seam. Press away from goose.

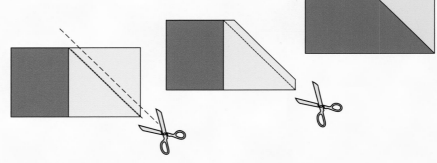

3 Repeat with second goose triangle square in opposite corner of goose. Press.

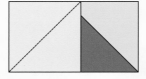 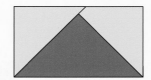

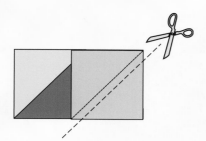

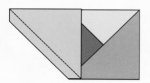 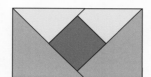

4 Mark sky squares on the wrong side with a diagonal line. Place one right side down on goose unit matching corners. Check that diagonal line is at right angles to original goose seam. Stitch on the marked diagonal line. Remove excess fabric leaving a ¼" seam. Press away from goose.

5 Repeat with second goose triangle square in the opposite corner of the goose unit, again checking the position of the diagonal line is at right angles to goose seam. Press away from the goose.

Details from Down on the Farm *by Sheila Marr (top) and* Best friends *by Dena Daniels (below)*

What if...

...you combine nosy, racing or even half and half geese with diamond geese?

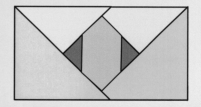

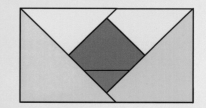

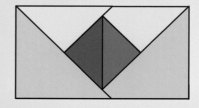

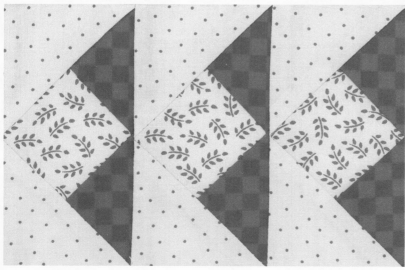

21

Half and half geese

Ideal for when you want to make the goose from two contrasting fabrics. Make two half square triangles and stitch them together to make a goose unit.

Easy cutting chart

Final width	Goose and sky
	Cut two squares in contrasting fabrics
4″	2⅞″ × 2⅞″
6″	3⅞″ × 3⅞″
8″	4⅞″ × 4⅞″

Quilt by Pippa Moss
(43″ × 52″)

1 Place a pair of contrasting squares right sides together. Mark a diagonal line on the wrong side of the lightest square.

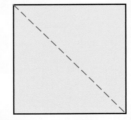

2 Stitch ¼″ away from the marked line. Sew one side of the line, pull the fabric squares away from the presser foot without breaking the thread, and then sew down the other side ¼″ away from the line. Press to bed the stitches.

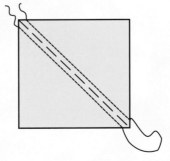

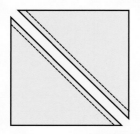
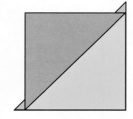
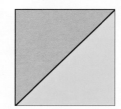

3 Cut on the marked line to divide the squares into two equal triangles.

4 Open each triangle to reveal a square containing two contrasting triangles.

5 Gently press the seam towards the darker fabric, taking care not to stretch the seam while you are pressing. Cut off the ears.

6 Stitch two different coloured half square triangles together to make one goose unit.

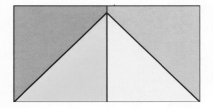

When joining, sew from the goose tip to help align the diagonal seams. If you find there is slippage then twist the top seam to 'nestle and wrestle' against the seam underneath.

Sea and Sand *by*
Karin Hellaby
(36" × 38")

QH tip

If you are making multiples of half and half geese consider cutting fabric first into strips and then into squares. Layering the goose and sky fabric right sides together before cutting will also fast fly those geese!

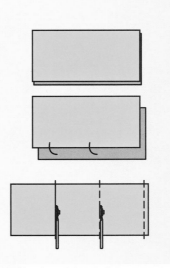

23

Pinwheel geese

Detail from Hearts in a Spin *by Ann Whatling (46" square)*

The pinwheel is made from four geese arranged to give a spinning look. Each cutting makes two pinwheels. If only one pinwheel is needed then the seams will only work as in the **What if...** diagram on the next page.

Easy cutting chart

Each cutting makes two pinwheels

Final pinwheel (4 geese)	Sky (cut squares)	Goose (cut 2 squares)
4"	$4 \times 2\frac{7}{8}"$ $2 \times 3\frac{1}{4}"$	$3\frac{1}{4}"$
6"	$4 \times 3\frac{7}{8}"$ $2 \times 4\frac{1}{4}"$	$4\frac{1}{4}"$
8"	$4 \times 4\frac{7}{8}"$ $2 \times 5\frac{1}{4}"$	$5\frac{1}{4}"$

1 Use one goose square and one equivalent sized sky square to make half square triangles (for more detailed instructions see page 222).

Place squares right sides together. Mark lightest square with a diagonal line from corner to corner. Stitch a ¼" seam either side of the centre marked line. Press.

Cut along centre marked line. Open up each triangle to make a square. Press to dark. Cut off 'ears'.

Repeat to make four half square triangles.

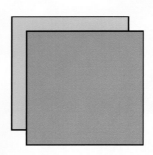

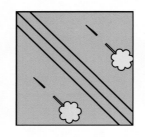

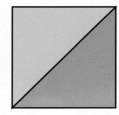

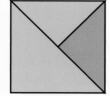

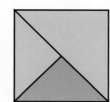

2 Draw a diagonal line on wrong side of small sky squares. Place a sky square right sides together with a half square triangle square. Check that marked line is positioned at right angles to the underneath seam line. Stitch each side of marked line. Press towards large sky square. Trim 'ears'. Repeat with remaining half square triangles.

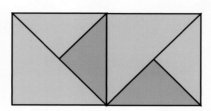

3 Stitch two squares together in pairs as shown. Check that seams are aligned as in diagram. Press centre seam towards the 'sky'.

4 Stitch four squares together to make one pinwheel. Press centre seam open to reduce bulk.

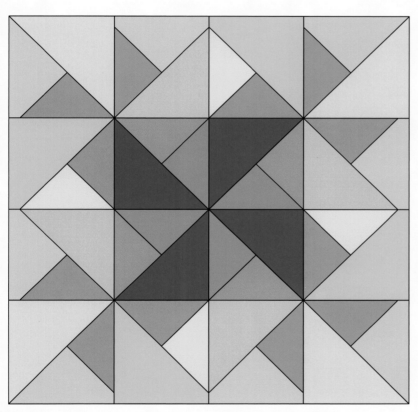

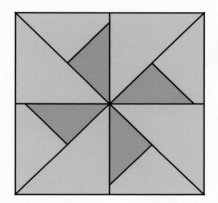

What if...

...you only need one pinwheel?

Follow stages 1 and 2, but stitch the blocks together as shown here.

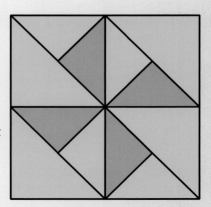

3D Geese

I love teaching this technique: it makes me feel like a magician! Try it, and you will see how this goose magically appears after only one seam has been sewn.

Loosen the Goose *by Annette Morgan* (39" × 44")

Easy cutting chart

Final width	Sky sq (2)	Goose (1)
4"	2½"	4½" × 2½"
6"	3½"	6½" × 3½"
8"	4½"	8½" × 4½"

1 Fold a goose fabric rectangle in half, right sides out. The fold must be in the centre of the long sides. Crease.

2 Place the folded goose onto the right side of a sky square, matching raw edges and corners. The fold will sit approximately ¼" inside the sky square. Pin.

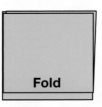
Fold

3 Place the second sky square on top, right sides down. The goose is now the filling between the sky squares. Pin.

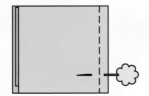

4 Sew one seam only. This seam must be at right angles to the fold of the goose.

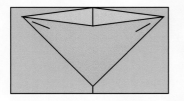
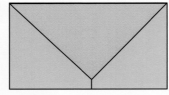

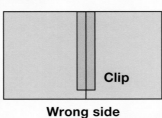

Clip

Wrong side

5 Open up the unit and press open the seam, positioning it centrally. Check that it is pressed evenly so that the goose looks balanced and the base of the goose is in line with the sky. Clip the goose seam tip so that it lies flat and open.

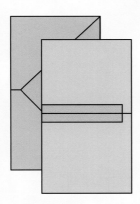

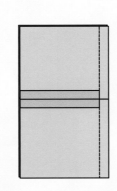

6 Stitch two geese together to make a pair by first laying them right side up and then flipping one goose over the other, right sides together.

Sew from the side of the clipped goose tip using the clipped seam as a guide for your seam line. This will help you retain a tip on your goose when the units are sewn together.

QH Tip

Tack or stay stitch the base of the goose before sewing geese together.

Raspberry Ripple by Heather Langdon
(49" square)

What if...

...you curved the geese sides – one side or both?

...you sewed two geese together along their base?

3D Half and half geese

3D helps to give the geese dimension and also allows you to curve the wings. Here we make geese that are divided from tip to base into two colours! Or try a more subtle effect by using two shades of one colour.

1 Stitch the two goose rectangles right sides together.

2 Press the seam open. Depending on finished size you now have either:
- a 2½″ × 4½″ rectangle (4″)
- or a 3½″ × 6½″ rectangle (6″)
- or a 4½″ × 8½″ rectangle (8″)

3 Fold the rectangle in half right sides out. Crease along the seam.

4 Place the folded goose onto the right side of a sky square, matching raw edges and corners. Make a note of which fabric is uppermost as this will decide which side it appears in the finished goose. The fold will be approximately ¼″ inside the square. Pin.

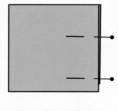

Fold

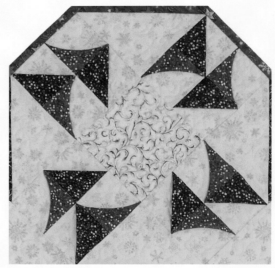

Easy cutting chart

Final width	Sky sq (2)	Goose (2)*
4″	2½″	2″ × 2½″
6″	3½″	2″ × 3½″
8″	4½″	2½″ × 4½″

*2 rectangles, one from each of two contrasting fabrics

5 Place the second sky square on top, right sides down. The goose is now the filling between the squares. Pin.

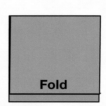

6 Sew one seam only. This seam must be at right angles to the fold of the goose. Start stitching from the end with four layers of fabric.

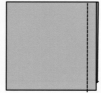

7 Press open the seam positioning it centrally. Check it is pressed evenly, so the goose looks balanced. On the reverse side pull apart the tip of the goose seam so that it lies flat and open.

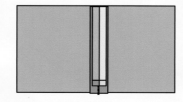
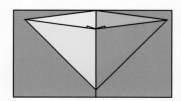

Curved wing geese

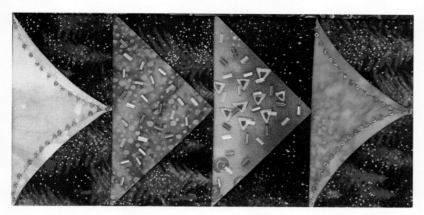

Take a sewn 3D goose unit (see page 26). Turn the goose sides up and over and stitch down to create curved wings. Allow the turning to fall into its natural shape. When straight stitching, start and finish ½″ in from tip and base just as the curve widens.

1 Catch down with a button or bead.

2 Catch down with a running stitch to look like quilting. You could consider doing this when quilting but you have the disadvantage of having to stitch through many layers.

3 Catch down with embroidery thread and stitches.

QH tip

Curved wing geese look more like a bird than the traditional patchwork shape. They look good in rows and in patchwork blocks. You can have geese and curved wing geese together in the same setting.

3D Diamond geese

1 Make a goose unit.

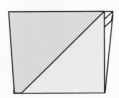

I really enjoy making this variation as it is simpler than the original diamond geese. Quick to make and very effective!

Easy cutting chart

Final width	Sky squares (2)	Goose
4"	2½"	2½" × 4½"
6"	3½"	3½" × 6½"
8"	4½"	4½" × 8½"

2 Fold goose unit in half as shown.

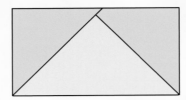

3 Place right sides together in between sky squares. Match raw edges and check that goose fold is ¼" away from top of sky squares.

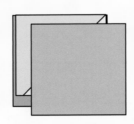

4 Stitch seam which must be at right angles to goose fold.

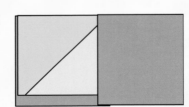

5 Press open the seam, positioning it centrally. Check that it is pressed evenly so that the goose looks balanced. On the reverse side pull apart the tip of the goose seam so that it lies flat and open.

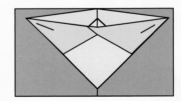

What if...

...you curve wing the goose?

...the original goose unit had two different sky fabrics, one on each side?

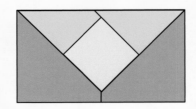

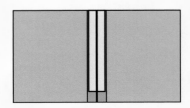

3D Nosy geese

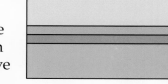

Easy cutting chart

Final width	Sky sq (2)	Goose*
4″	2½″	1½″ × 4½″
6″	3½″	2″ × 6½″
8″	4½″	2½″ × 8½″

*Cut two rectangles, one from each of two contrasting fabrics.

1 Stitch the two goose rectangles right sides together, sewing along the longer side. Depending on finished size you now have either:
- a 2½″ × 4½″ rectangle (4″)
- or a 3½″ × 6½″ rectangle (6″)
- or a 4½″ × 8½″ rectangle (8″)

2 Press the seam open.

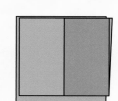

3 Fold the rectangle in half right sides out. Crease.

4 Place the folded goose onto the right side of a sky square, matching raw edges and corners. Make a note of which goose fabric is sewn into the seam, as this will be the fabric that forms the goose tip or nose. The fabric fold will be approximately ¼″ inside the square. Pin.

5 Place the second sky square on top, right sides down. The goose is now the filling between the squares. Pin.

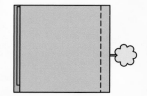

6 Sew one seam only. This seam must be at right angles to the fold of the goose. Start stitching from the end with four layers of fabric.

7 Press open the seam, positioning it centrally. Check that it is pressed evenly so that the goose looks balanced. On the reverse side pull apart the tip of the goose seam so that it lies flat and open.

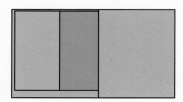

What if...

...you make the widths of the rectangles unequal?

...you vary the size of the geese?

3D Racing geese

1 Make a rectangle with the three goose rectangles by placing the centre rectangle in the middle and the two remaining rectangles on either side of it.

Stitch, right sides together, sewing along the longer sides. Press open. Depending on finished size you now have either:
- a 2½″ × 4½″ rectangle (4″)
- or a 3½″ × 6½″ rectangle (6″)
- or a 4½″ × 8½″ rectangle (8″)

Easy cutting chart

Final width	Sky square (2)	Goose centre	Goose sides (2)
4″	2½″	2″ × 2½″	1¾″ × 2½″
6″	3½″	2″ × 3½″	2¾″ × 3½″
8″	4½″	2½″× 4½″	3½″ × 4½″

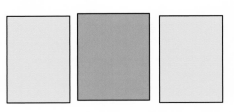 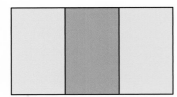

2 Press the seams open.

3 Fold the rectangle in half right sides out. Crease.

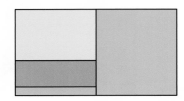

4 Place the folded goose onto the right side of a sky square, matching raw edges and corners. The fabric fold will be approximately ¼″ inside the square. Pin.

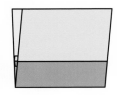

5 Place the second sky square on top, right side down. The goose is now the filling between the squares. Pin.

6 Sew one seam only. This seam must be at right angles to the fold of the goose. Start stitching from the end with four layers of fabric.

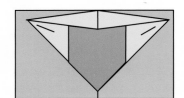

7 Press open the seam, positioning it centrally. Check that it is pressed evenly so that the goose looks balanced. Clip the tip of the goose seam so that it lies flat and open.

What if...

...all three goose sections were made up of different fabrics?

...you 'curved wing' some of these units?

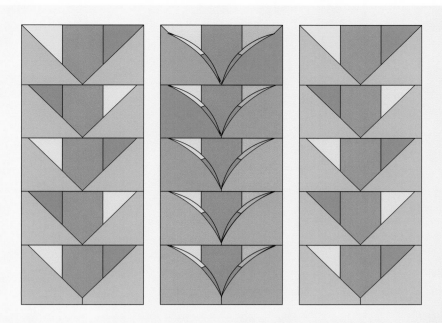

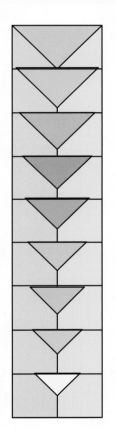
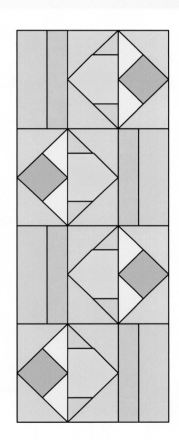
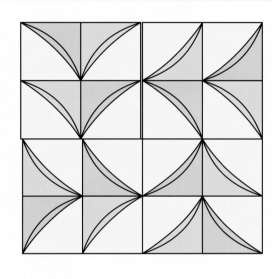
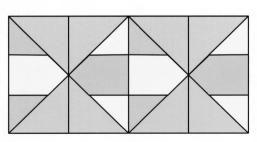
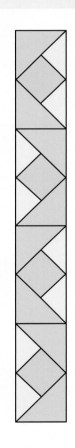

3D geese can be combined and experimented with in many exciting ways. Here are a few ideas to try.

Flying geese no waste

Tropical flocks *by*
Karin Hellaby (55" × 64")

This method is brilliant! Not only does it eliminate the need to cut out triangles and stitch along stretchy bias edges but there is no wastage of fabric.

Easy cutting chart

Final width	Sky sq (4)	Goose sq (1)*
4"	2⅞"	5¼"
6"	3⅞"	7¼"
8"	4⅞"	9¼"

*Each time you cut and sew you make four geese!

1 Place large goose square right side up and lay two small sky squares exactly in opposite corners wrong sides up. Match raw edges.

2 Where the sky squares cross each other in the centre, trim the overlapping corners. Use a ruler to mark a straight line diagonally from corner to corner on the small squares. Pin.

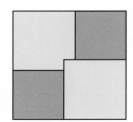

3 Stitch a ¼" seam on both sides of the diagonal line.

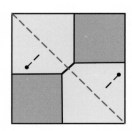

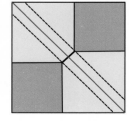

4 Cut apart on the centre marked line between the stitch lines.

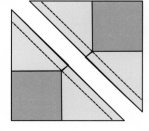

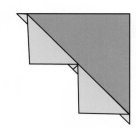

5 Gently press the sky triangles away from the goose.

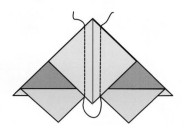

6 Draw a diagonal line on the wrong side of the remaining two sky squares. Right sides together pin one into the 'empty' corner on the goose and stitch a ¼" seam on both sides of the marked line. Repeat with the remaining half goose section.

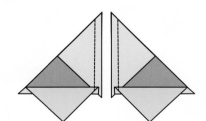

7 Cut apart on the centre marked line between the stitch lines.

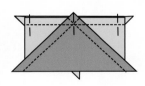
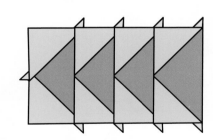

8 Press the four geese carefully, using the side of the iron to avoid distortion. The sky should be pressed away from the goose.

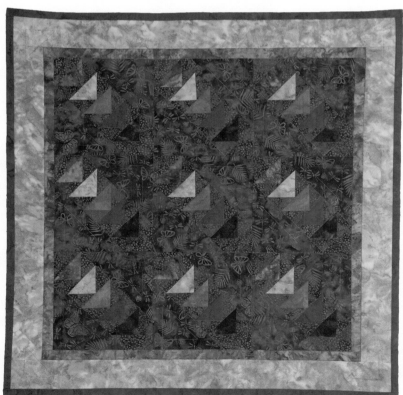

Turkish Delight *by*
Susan Prior
(38" × 38")

Migrating geese no waste

When I first included this technique in **Sew a Row Quilts** it was instantly popular because nobody had seen it before. This time I have included a 6″ size to play with. New instructions are given for finishing the row.

Easy cutting chart

Final width	Sky sq (2)	Goose sq*
4″	3⅝″	3⅞″
6″	4⅞″	5¼″
8″	6¼″	6⅝″

*makes three geese – cut one

Flower Flight 2 *by*
Pam Bailey
(54″ × 64″)

1 Cut the goose square in half diagonally from corner to corner.

2 Right sides together, lay one goose triangle in the corner of a sky square, matching raw edges. Pin.

3 Stitch a ¼″ seam around the two sides of the triangle, turning on the diagonal line by leaving the needle inserted and then lifting the presser foot before you turn the corner.

4 Cut in half diagonally through the centre of the triangle. You will now have a right and a left goose unit. Press each goose away from the sky. Cut off 'ears'.

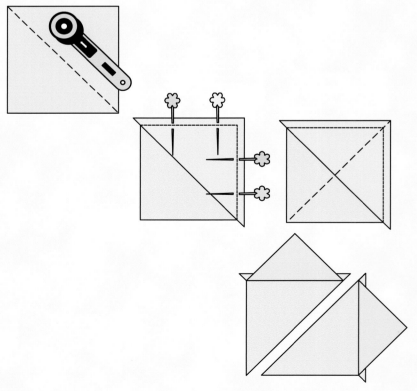

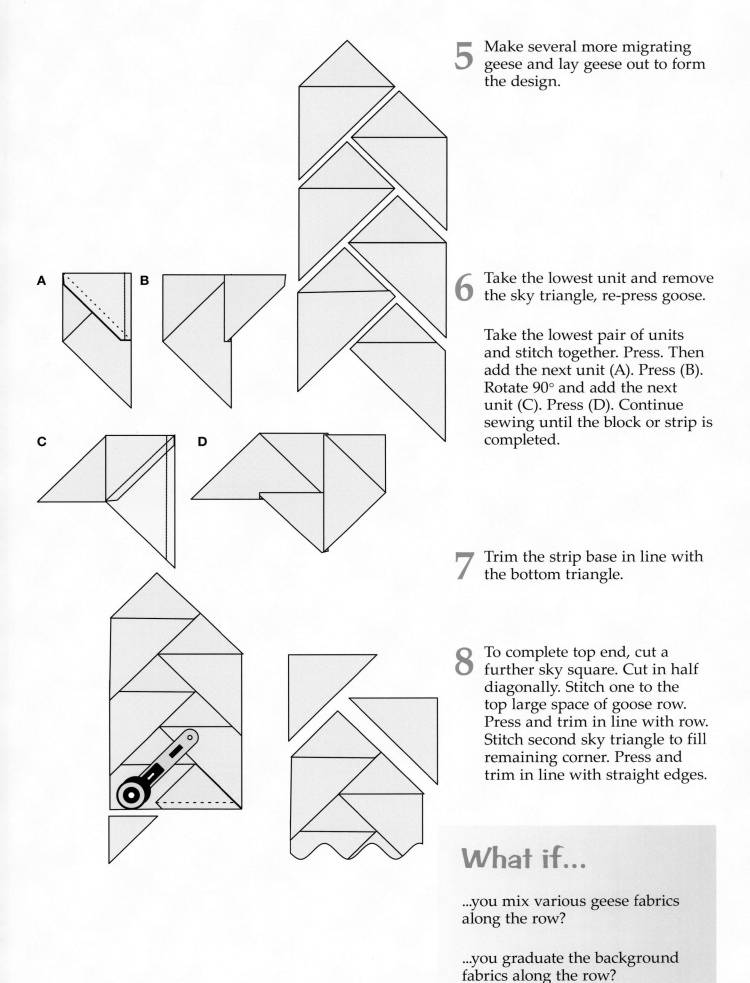

5 Make several more migrating geese and lay geese out to form the design.

6 Take the lowest unit and remove the sky triangle, re-press goose.

Take the lowest pair of units and stitch together. Press. Then add the next unit (A). Press (B). Rotate 90° and add the next unit (C). Press (D). Continue sewing until the block or strip is completed.

7 Trim the strip base in line with the bottom triangle.

8 To complete top end, cut a further sky square. Cut in half diagonally. Stitch one to the top large space of goose row. Press and trim in line with row. Stitch second sky triangle to fill remaining corner. Press and trim in line with straight edges.

What if...

...you mix various geese fabrics along the row?

...you graduate the background fabrics along the row?

Migrating from recs and squares

The challenge here was to take the popular migrating geese and find some fun variations. Once you have mastered this one you can use it to migrate the racing, nosy and diamond variations.

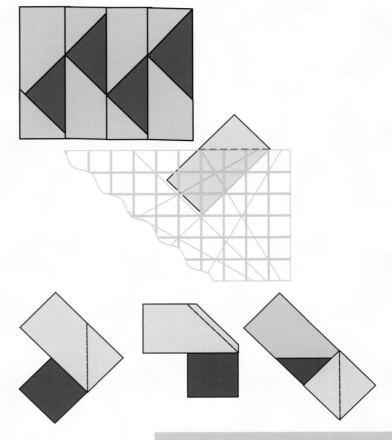

1 On wrong side of sky rectangle draw a diagonal line from one corner using the 45° line on fabric edge.

2 Place right sides together and at right angles with goose rectangle, matching raw edges. Pin and check that the sky folds back into the correct position. Stitch on the drawn line. Remove excess seam allowance and press away from the goose.

3 On wrong side of sky square draw a diagonal line from corner to corner.

Easy cutting chart

Final width	Sky sq	Sky rectangle	Goose
4″	2½″	2½″×4½″	2½″ × 4½″
6″	3½″	3½″×6½″	3½″ × 6½″
8″	4½″	4½″×8½″	4½″ × 8½″

4 Place sky square at other side of goose rectangle, right sides together and matching raw edges. Stitch on line. Trim away excess seam allowance and press away from goose.

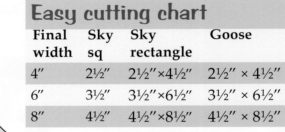

5 Stitch more goose units, stitching half with goose towards one side and half with goose towards the other side. To do this you will only need to alter the sky rectangle stitching line, drawing the alternate line from the opposite corner. Stitch together using alternate units.

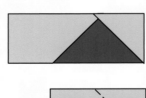

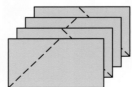

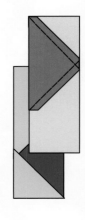

3D Migrating geese

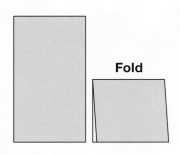

Fold

This is very clever but so easy! The technique can be used for 3D migrating versions of racing, diamond and nosy geese. Of course you can curve them, too!

1 Fold the goose (right side out) in half across the width.

2 Place right side to right side on the sky rectangle, matching raw edges on one side and base. Goose fold will be positioned ¼″ from top of sky.

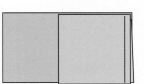

3 Place sky square on top of goose right sides together, matching raw edges.

4 Stitch along the short side.

Easy cutting chart

Final width	Sky sq	Sky rectangle	Goose
4″	2½″	2½″×4½″	2½″ × 4½″
6″	3½″	3½″×6½″	3½″ × 6½″
8″	4½″	4½″×8½″	4½″ × 8½″

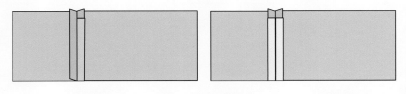

5 Open up the unit and press open the seam. Check that it is pressed evenly so that the goose base is even with the sky base. Clip the tip of the goose seam so that it lies flat and open.

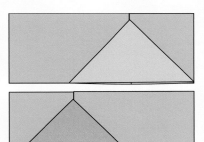

6 Make 3D goose units, alternating the sky side.

7 Join the geese together to make a block or a row.

QH tip

To join geese and leave perfect tips, take one right and one left goose unit. Lay right sides together so geese 'snuggle' alongside each other. Pin and stitch from side that shows you where to 'hit' the ¼″ seam allowance. Press joining seam away from goose tip.

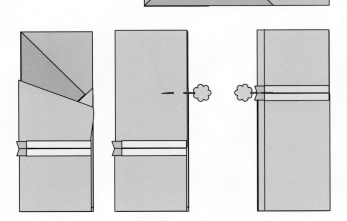

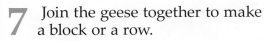

Prairie geese

Take a square of fabric and fold into a goose. Then find lots of fascinating ways to use these prairie geese to give dimension to your patchwork.

Easy cutting chart

Final width	Final height	Sky (1)	Goose sq (1)
4″	2″	2½″ × 4½″	4½″
6″	3″	3½″ × 6½″	6½″
8″	4″	4½″ × 8½″	8½″

Detail of Gift Tree
by Theresa Wardlaw

1 Fold the square in half, right sides out into a rectangle. Press.

2 Fold sides in towards centre, as shown in diagram, and press.

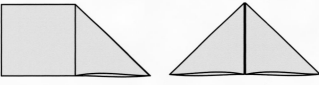

3 Place folded goose onto right side of sky rectangle. Pin and tack into position along the goose base. Stitch goose tip down onto sky fabric.

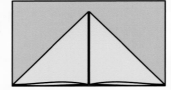

What if...

...you use a graduated fabric for your prairie geese?

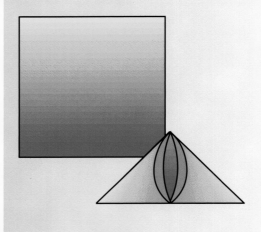

4 Stitch several prairie geese into a row or block.

5 Insert between strips of fabric.

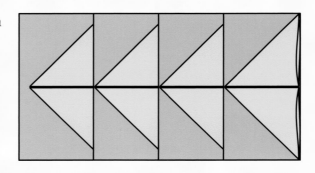

Crazy geese 1

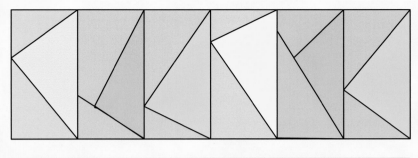

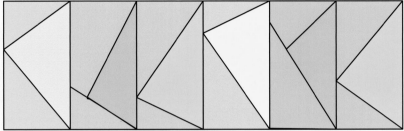

Inspired by Jan Mullen whose crazy work and wonderful bright fabrics I have admired for many years. These crazy geese are ideal for those who dislike accurate cutting and stitching and prefer not to work on a foundation. Can you imagine these marching around a border?

Easy cutting chart

Final width	Sky square (1)	Goose (1)
4″	4″	2½″ × 4½″
6″	6″	3½″ × 6½″
8″	8″	4½″ × 8½″

1   Cut the sky square into two triangles by making one diagonal cut.

2   Place goose right side up. Place one sky triangle right side up on the goose to roughly cover a corner area. Flip the triangle over, pulling it back ¼″ towards the corner to allow for the seam allowance and to ensure it will eventually cover the corner. Pin on seam line, flip so that you can check that the triangle covers the corner of the goose completely. Both pieces should be right sides together before stitching the seam.

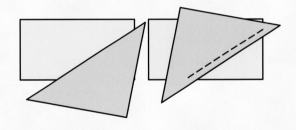

3   Press the triangle away from the goose.

4   Now trim the triangle in line with the edges of the goose in order to keep to the original size. To do this easily simply place the unit right sides down on your cutting mat, place your ruler on the goose edge and trim away the excess fabric.

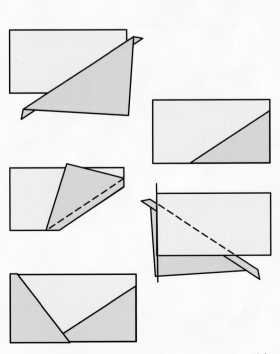

5   Pull back the triangle and trim away the excess goose fabric.

6   Repeat for the other side, again varying the sky area.

Crazy geese 2

Ideal for beginners who wish to try foundation piecing for the first time. This is an accurate method for stitching various shaped geese as you stitch on the drawn line.

1 Draw goose rectangle onto soluble paper, a thin foundation paper or an easy tear vilene.

2 Label the goose 1 and sky areas 2 & 3.

3 Choose fabric and cut a patch approximately 1″ larger than the goose area.

4 Repeat with the sky fabric.

5 When sewing on a foundation, the stitching is always done from the printed side of the paper, but the fabric is placed on the unprinted side.

Place the goose patch right side up over patch 1 on the unprinted side. Check that patch 1 is completely covered by fabric by holding the foundation up to the light. Pin in place from the printed side.

6 With the foundation right side up, place a piece of card along the line that separates patch 1 and patch 2. Fold the foundation paper back on the line, and hook an add-a-quarter ruler onto the fold so that the ¼″ lip is pushed against it. Trim the exposed fabric by rotary cutting along the add-a-quarter ruler, leaving a ¼″ fabric seam allowance. Alternatively, you can use a rotary ruler to trim ¼″ from the fold.

Final width	Paper rectangle
4″	2″ × 4″
6″	3″ × 6″
8″	4″ × 8″

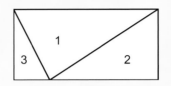

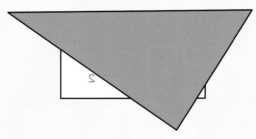

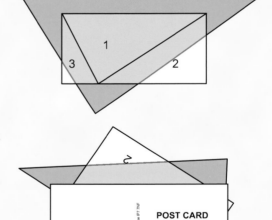

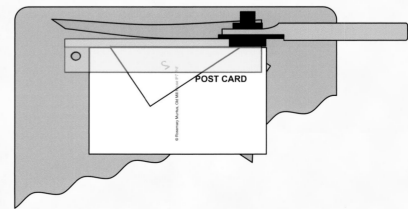

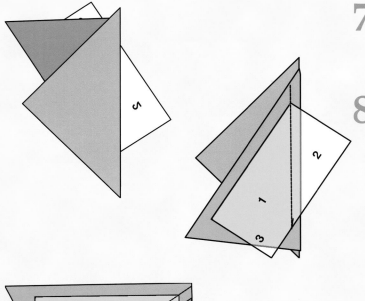

7 Turn fabric side up and with right sides together correctly position sky fabric patch 2 so that one straight edge matches the trimmed edge. Pin from the printed side.

8 Machine sew on the printed side exactly on the line that separates patch 1 and 2. An open toed or clear plastic machine foot helps as you will be able to see the line as you sew. Change your machine needle to a larger size 90/14 which will make larger holes in the paper foundation, helping you to tear it away later. Use a short machine stitch (15 stitches per inch) to help perforate the paper.

Start stitching two or three stitches before the start of your sewing line, and extend your stitching by a few stitches past the line.

9 On the fabric side press sky fabric 2 over patch 2.

10 Repeat with sky fabric to cover patch 3. Press and your goose is complete.

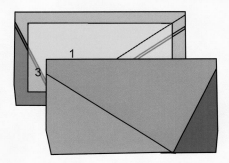

11 Trim the goose unit ¼" from the outside line to give you a seam allowance.

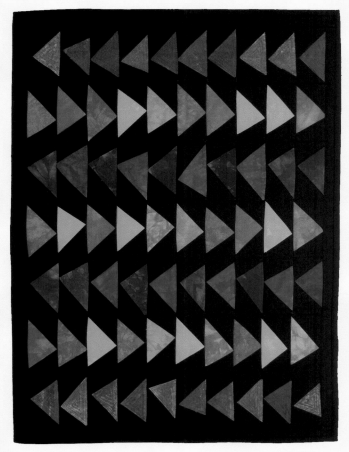

Crazy Geese by Lin Patterson (22" × 30")

QH tip

Half-inch pins are ideal for pinning foundation paper as they are small enough to do the job without getting in the way of stitching.

Logs and geese

Detail from
Poppy Power *by*
Erica Ransom

Now things start to get really exciting, but this goose block is much easier than you might think. Great trees and other designs emerge when extra strips (logs) are added to the 'goose'. One block has two units as shown alongside.

Easy cutting chart

Block size	Logs (4)	Sky sq (2)	Goose: (1)
6"	1½" × 5"	3¾"	4¼"
8"	2" × 7"	4¾"	5¼"

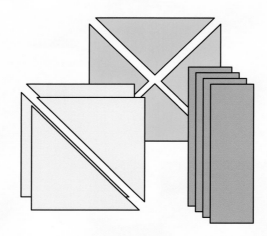

1 Cut goose square into four triangles using two diagonal cuts. Cut sky squares into two triangles.

2 Place one log alongside a goose triangle, right sides up. Flip over, aligning corner to corner and stitch with ¼" seam. Press away from goose.

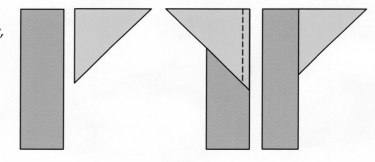

3 Place second log alongside goose other side, right sides up. Flip over, aligning corners and stitch with ¼" seam. Press away from goose. You now have a log on the two side edges of the goose.

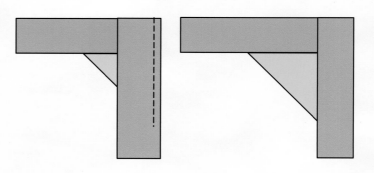

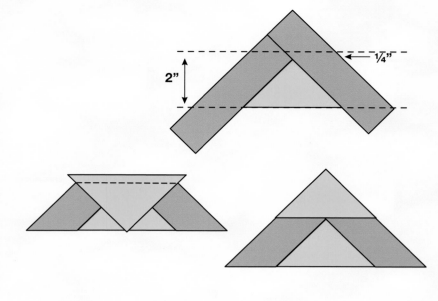

4 Trim away excess log fabric from base goose. Trim unit tip 2" from base of goose, checking first that you have a ¼" seam allowance from tip of goose. (2½" for 8" block).

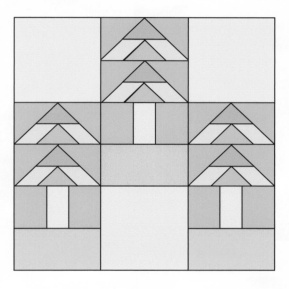

5 Stitch a second goose to the top of the first logged goose. Press seam towards second goose.

Another design using logs and geese

QH tip

Crease goose in half, point to tip and, then match crease to tip of first goose.

Trim any excess from log sides so that they are in line with top goose.

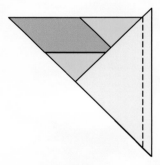

6 Cut a sky square in half diagonally. Stitch to sides of goose unit to form a rectangle. Press.

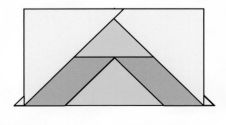

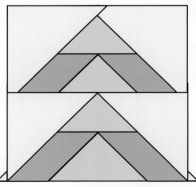

7 Repeat to make a second goose rectangle.

8 Stitch rectangles together into a block.

45

Geese behind the scenes

Geese making a spectacular appearance behind the scenes in Wild Geese *by Theresa Wardlaw (21" × 41").*

This technique is ideal for using those fantastic fabrics that change colour, or shade, from end to end. It works best when you have a night sky, because a dark fabric helps to hide any seams.

A reverse appliqué technique is used to reveal the geese behind the top layer.

Decorative threads and stitches can be used to emphasise the shapes, which can be any size you like (and curved or crazy as well)!

1 Draw a line of geese onto the matt side of a piece of freezer paper. If you choose to draw your own design make sure you have closed areas for the geese and that the geese link together for easy sewing.

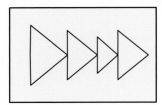

QH tip

You may find it easier to draw the geese using a folded piece of paper to draw one half of the geese before turning over to trace the other half.

2 You will need two pieces of fabric. The top fabric will be the 'sky' and should be the size of the area in which the geese are 'found ', this could be as large as your quilt top, a block, or a row. The second fabric will become the geese and underneath layer. This does not need to be the same size as the sky fabric, but it will need to be larger than the area in which the geese appear.

What if...

...you freehand draw the pattern onto the right side of the sky fabric to eliminate the need for a freezer paper pattern?

3 Iron the glossy side of the freezer paper pattern to the right side of the sky fabric.

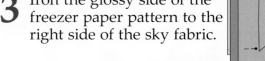

QH tip

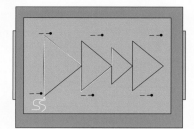

When revealing the geese, nip the top layer of fabric between your thumb and forefinger and make a small cut. Release and then place your scissors in the cut to trim.

4 Pin the goose fabric, right side up, under the sky fabric beneath the drawn geese. Both fabrics will be right side up, with the goose fabric right side to wrong side of the sky fabric.

5 Set your machine stitch to a small straight stitch (about 15 stitches to the inch).

6 Stitch with a continuous line, following the pencilled geese lines on the freezer paper.

7 Gently remove the freezer paper.

Admire those wonderful coloured geese as they appear from 'behind the scenes'

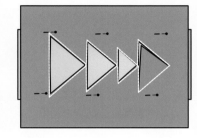

8 Use a sharp pair of small scissors to cut away the top fabric only within the geese shapes to within $1/16''$ of the stitching.

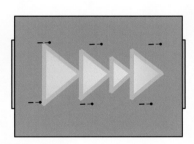

9 Use a satin stitch, decorative stitch or couch embellishing threads to cover the raw edges of the geese, following the continuous line from goose to goose.

Butterflies by Debs Gardiner (40" × 56")

47

Geese in flight

Inspired by the work of Carol Bryer Fallert, this is a method I have devised so you can draft your own designs. If you wish you can try the pattern on page 87.

Detail from Angel Serenade *by Julia Reed from an original doodle by Karin Hellaby* (46" × 46")

1 Cut out and or tape together freezer paper to the size of the finished quilt (or area of the quilt) in which you wish to piece geese in flight.

2 Draw a line incorporating one or two gentle curves.

3 Draw a second line running parallel to (or just alongside) the first, and approximately 3–6" away from it. Label each main section. Draw a rough sketch showing main areas and duplicate markings.

4 Draw a dashed line between the two original lines (this will act as a reference point for the tips of the geese).

5 Draw geese flying in one direction. They can be squat or tall. It does not matter that each one is slightly different. Use the centre dashed line as a guide to place the centre tip of each goose.

6 If you wish you can draw a second or third flight of geese, using the technique described.

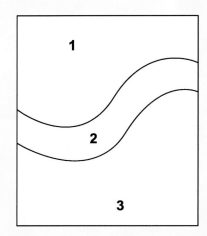

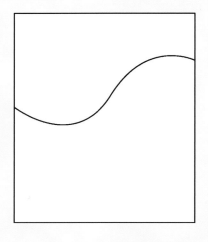

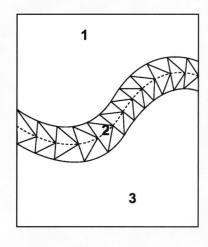

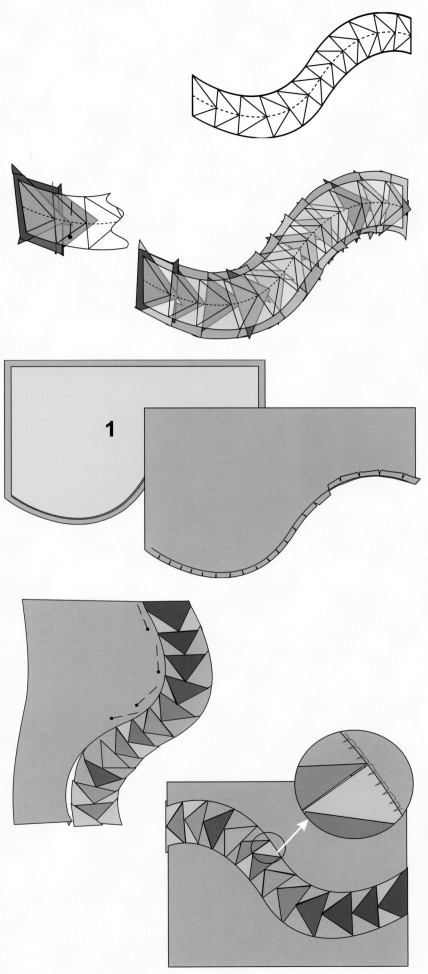

7 Cut out whole section of geese in flight – you do not cut out the individual geese.

8 Choose fabric and cut a patch 1″ larger than the first goose. If you are using the same fabric for all the geese then measure the largest goose and cut a strip of fabric 1″ wider. This strip can then be cut into smaller units for each goose as you sew. Repeat with the sky fabric.

9 Using the same foundation piecing method as for crazy piecing on page 42, stitch the line of geese from the base end to the point end. Gently remove freezer paper.

10 Iron large freezer paper section to reverse of background fabric. Cut out adding a ¼″ seam allowance all round. Stay stitch curved edge (i.e. the edge that will join the geese section).

11 Clip the seam allowance to the stay stitches without cutting into them. Clip every ¼″–½″. Remove freezer paper. Gently press under the seam allowance with the stay stitching line just under the pressed edge. Lay the background sections overlapping geese section to cover geese seam allowance. Tack or pin in place. Make sure you keep those beautiful points on the geese! Stitch in place using hand appliqué stitches. Repeat with background section 3.

QH tip

The sections can be joined using machine stitching using a blind hem or decorative stitch. You could also consider couching a thicker embroidery thread.

Geese in a circle

Drafting your own pattern

It's really easy to draft your own pattern for Geese in a Circle, and that way you can choose to make the circle any size you like, create geese of any size, and have as many as you like flying inside your circle! The diagrams on these pages will give you 16 plump geese. You could have leaner ones if you fold the paper once more to create 32 geese (as in the quilt on the left).

Christmas Wreath
by Heather Langdon
(28" square)

1 Using a pair of compasses or a C-thru ruler (holes at ½" intervals down centre) draw a circle on freezer paper. Start with a circle between 6–8" in radius, and mark the centre point.

2 Draw an inner circle 2–3" smaller than the outer circle. Draw a third circle using a dashed line half way between the original two circles.

3 Cut out exactly on the drawn outer circle.

4 Fold the circle to create spokes radiating from the centre. Each spoke will become a goose so fold as many times as you wish. If you are creating more than 16 spokes you may wish to open up your circle and refold between the original spokes to prevent the paper becoming too bulky.

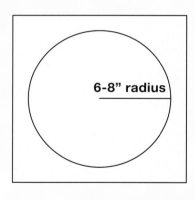

6-8" radius

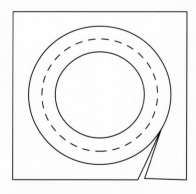

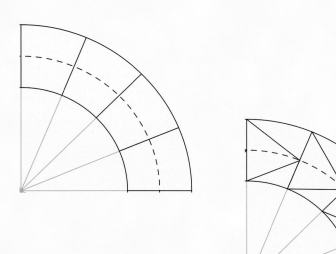

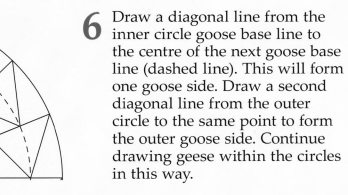

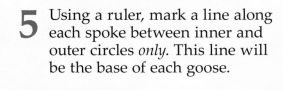

5 Using a ruler, mark a line along each spoke between inner and outer circles *only*. This line will be the base of each goose.

6 Draw a diagonal line from the inner circle goose base line to the centre of the next goose base line (dashed line). This will form one goose side. Draw a second diagonal line from the outer circle to the same point to form the outer goose side. Continue drawing geese within the circles in this way.

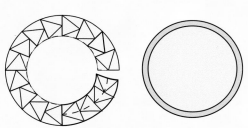

7 Cut out inner circle and iron onto the wrong side of the chosen centre fabric. Cut out with ⅜″ seam allowance. Gather ¼″ from the edge by machine or by hand. Pull the gathering thread and thumb press the edge of the fabric carefully over your paper circle. Set aside until needed for centre fabric appliqué.

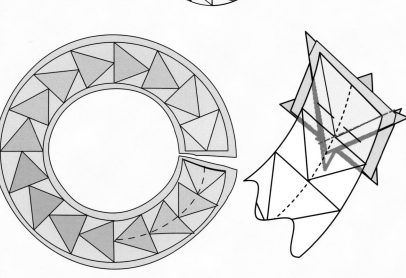

8 Fabric stitch the goose pattern, referring to the instructions on page 49.

9 Appliqué centre circle in place. Insert circle of geese into a background fabric following instructions on page 9.

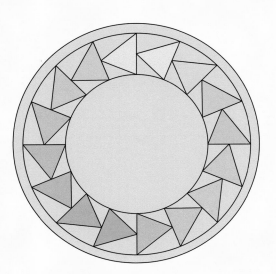

No sew geese

No sew appliqué

No sew appliqué appeals to those who love the look of appliqué but do not wish to stitch the appliqués. Sometimes sewn and no sew appliqués are used in the same piece of work.

I use Steam-a-seam 2, a no-sew fusible which has a pressure sensitive adhesive allowing me to position the goose shapes on my background fabric while it is hanging vertically on a design wall! When I am happy with the design, I simply iron the shapes to bond them in position. No further sewing is needed as the fused fabric edges should not fray even after gentle hand washing. If you decide to use other heavyweight fusible webs, read the manufacturer's instructions carefully.

Raw edge appliqué

For this technique I like to use loose weave fabrics such as Homespuns.

You can choose to freely draw and cut a goose shape or if you wish to make them more uniform in size then cut a square of fabric in four with two diagonal cuts to make four geese. Pin the goose in position onto the background fabric and stitch down using ⅛" seam allowance from raw edge. You may decide to use a decorative stitch at this stage.

When you have completed all the stitching place the quilt top in a tumble drier for a short while to fluff up the raw edges.

Above: Windmills of my Mind *by Christine Davies (50" square).*

Right: detail of Sunflowers on Parade *by Grace Howes, North Carolina (39" × 52")*

Raw edge geese in a pinwheel block

Cut four 4½" squares (sky). Cut one 4½" square in a contrast colour, divide into four triangles (geese) using two diagonal cuts. Place one goose right side up, on top of a sky square with its long edges together. Stitch ⅛" along two shorter sides of goose. Repeat with remaining geese. Stitch four geese into a pinwheel block.

Pinwheel block by Karin Hellaby

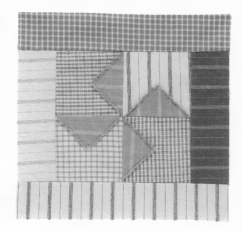

Valentine's Day was very much on my mind when I designed this quilt. Kissing geese alternate with a heart inside a heart block and quilted hearts flying all over the quilt!

Fabric needed

Background (cream) – 2 yards

Background (beige) – 1 yard

Cream heart centres (two fabrics) – ½ yard of each

Cream/red for kissing geese (two fabrics) – ¼ yard of each

Red roses – 1½ yards; red hearts – 1½ yards (kissing geese, geese border and geese hearts)

Borders and binding – 1½ yards

Cutting

- Cream background. Cut nine 8½" squares; 200 × 2½" squares, 22 × 4½" squares.

- Beige – cut eight 8½" squares; eighteen 4½" squares.

- Cream/red – cut three 2½" strips in each fabric.

- Red roses – cut three 2½" strips; eight large hearts (using template); fifty 2½" × 4½" rectangles.

- Red hearts – cut three 2½" strips; nine large hearts (using template); fifty 2½" × 4½" rectangles; four corner hearts.

- Cream heart centres (two fabrics) – cut eight small hearts (using template) in one fabric and nine small hearts in second fabric.

- Red borders – cut six 1½" strips (inner border); cut eight 4½" strips (outer border), cut six 2½" strips for binding.

Instructions

1 Kissing geese

Use instructions on page 16 for nosy geese. Stitch 2½" strips in reds and cream/red along the length in pairs. From the six pairs, cut eighteen 8½" × 4½" rectangles from each colourway. Use 4½" background squares to complete the geese. Stitch together in pairs to make an 8½" square. Make 18 kissing geese squares.

54

Be my Valentine (58" × 74") was designed by Karin Hellaby and made by Maggie Lamb, Heather Langdon and Karin Hellaby. Machine quilting is by Jan Chandler.

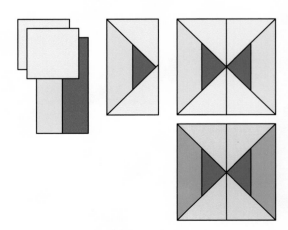

2 Large hearts

Appliqué a large heart to the centre of the 8½" cream and beige squares. Choose your favourite appliqué method or use a machine satin stitch, as we have done on this quilt. You will find templates for all the hearts on the next page.

3 Small hearts

Appliqué a small heart to the centre of the large heart.

4 Corner hearts

Appliqué four red corner hearts to the centre of four 4½" squares.

5 Recs and squares geese

Make 50 recs and squares geese using 4" instructions on page 15 in each of two colourways (100 geese altogether) for flying geese border. Stitch together 29 geese for each side border. Stitch together 21 geese each for the top and bottom borders, and stitch a heart square to each end.

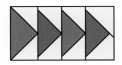

6 Finishing

Assemble the quilt centre, referring to the diagram and the quilt photograph. Add red 1½" border strips, flying geese borders, and red 4½" strips for outer border. Quilt (using the quilting patterns on the next page, if you wish) and bind.

I love cats

The same large and medium sized hearts are used here to create a rather different, smaller quilt: *I Love Cats* by Julia Reed (40" square). The dark fabric of the larger hearts creates a purrfect frame for an interesting feline fabric.

Quilting patterns and templates for
Be my Valentine *on page 53*

Geese in a snowstorm

Charlotte Ridler designed and made this fast moving quilt. Although at first it looks complicated, it is deceptively simple to make! How about using the blocks for a sandstorm or whirlwind?

57

Fabric needed

Blue background – 2 yards

Geese – ½ yard each of four cream/white fabrics

Cutting

- Background – cut 16 × 4½″ squares. Cut 224 × **2½″** squares. Cut three 13″ blocks. Cut two 7½″ blocks. Cut five 2½″ strips for binding.

- Geese Creams – cut eight 4½″ × 8½″ rectangles. Cut 112 2½″ × 4½″ rectangles.

Geese in a snowstorm *by Charlotte Ridler (34″ × 46″)*

Instructions

1 Centre four blocks

Stitch eight 8″ 3D geese following directions on page 26. Stitch into pairs to make four 8″ blocks. Create curved wing geese by pulling side edges back and holding with a centre stitch.

2 Small geese blocks

Each block is made from eight 3D geese.

Following the instructions on page 26 stitch 112 3D geese. Stitch geese into pairs. (Note that in this block only the lower goose of each pair is curved. Stitch geese pairs into an 8″ block as shown in diagram, to create a circle formation at the centre.

Make 14 × 8″ blocks.

QH Tip

L eave the wing curving until you assemble the quilt and use the stitches you sew to 'tie' the quilt.

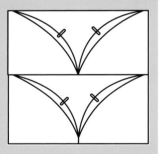

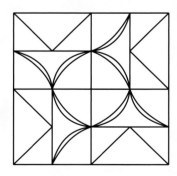

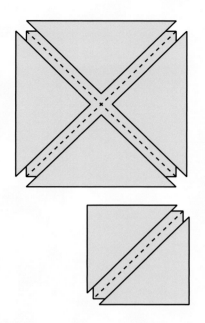

3 Making up the quilt top

Side triangles. Use the 13″ blocks. Divide into four triangles by making two diagonal cuts.

Corner triangle. Use the two 7½″ blocks. Divide into triangles with one diagonal cut.

Stitch blocks into rows as shown, adding the appropriate triangle to each end.

Stitch rows into the quilt top. Trim edges to lie straight and ½″ from tips of geese.

Layer. Quilt snowflake designs and add snowflake buttons.

Bind with a 1″ finished binding.

Geese in a sandstorm by Jean Minns (34″ × 46″) shows another way of assembling the same blocks, using a very different combination of colours.

QH Tips

Take care that you keep side and corner triangles separate, as it is important that the bias (stretchy) edge is used correctly.

Use buttons to tie the layers of the quilt together.

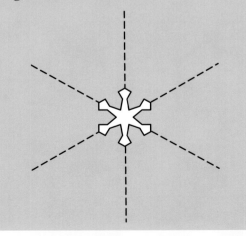

Gracie in a spin

As soon as we saw this quilt we knew it was a candidate for the front cover. Julia Reed designed and made the 41" square quilt, adding the charming Gracie to the centre.

Two circles of geese were stitched on a foundation paper and finally the free flying geese were hand appliquéd to the background.

Fabric needed

Goose – one obese eighth yard (11″ × 9″)
Goose bill and feet – scrap of yellow
Twelve colours – one obese eighth yard each
Background and binding – 2 yards

Cutting

Outer geese: cut four 4½″ × 2½″ rectangles in each colour. Inner geese: cut four 4½″ × 1¾″ rectangles in each colour. Stray geese: cut 23 more outer geese. You will also need 192 triangles of varying sizes in the background colour (see pages 50–51). Background: cut one 40″ square and four 1½″ strips for binding.

Instructions

Julia decided to make her ring of geese 28″ wide. She drew a quarter circle with a 14″ radius, then marked off 3½″ for the outer circle and another 3½″ for the inner circle.

She used protractor and ruler to create the geese, (twelve outer and twelve inner). You can modify this and create eight geese per quarter if you use the folding method given on page 50. This produces slightly bigger geese.

She used a photocopier to create three copies of her plan, then joined them in pairs and cut out the arcs, which she numbered and foundation pieced.

For the goose shape Julia used a simplified version of a sketch done for her by a local Essex artist, Tom Abrahams. They are both happy for the simplified version to be copied for personal use.

For fuller, more detailed instructions see Geese in a Circle on pages 50–51.

Central circle

Fold

Fold

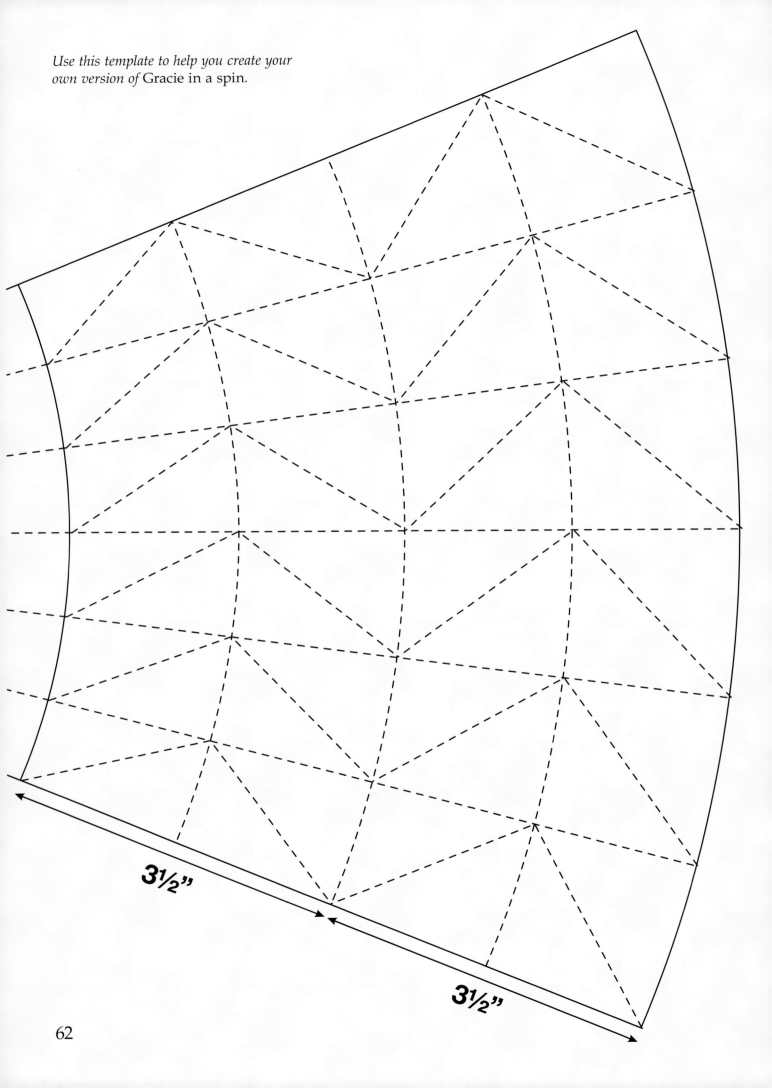

Use this template to help you create your own version of Gracie in a spin.

3½"

3½"

The Night they invented Champagne by Charlotte Ridler (35" × 38")

Who would have thought the nosy geese shape could make such fun champagne glasses? The cork popping in the bottom corner and the bead and stitchery embellishment add to the theme. How about making your own version of this quilt to celebrate an anniversary and ask each of your guests to sign a glass?

63

Fabric needed

Background black – 1½ yards

Blue/grey glasses – ½ yard

Pink bubbles – 1 yard

Cutting

- Background – cut 54 × 3½" squares; cut six 3½" background strips for stems; cut six 3½" × 6½" rectangles; cut three 3½" strips for borders.

- Blue/grey – cut two 2" strips and two 1½" strips for nosy geese; cut three 7/8" strips for stems.

- Pink – cut two 2" strips and two 2½" strips for nosy geese.

Instructions

1 Champagne glasses

Using instructions on page 16 make 27 nosy flying geese. Use the 6" finished measurement. Vary the width of the 'noses' if you wish.

Make 27 stems by inserting a ⅞" strip of blue/grey fabric between two 3½" background strips. Stitch three strip sets using ¼" seams. Press away from centre stem. Trim strip set to a 6½" width, keeping the 'stem' central.

Cut 27 3½" × 6½" rectangles. Join each 'nosy goose' to a 'stem' to make 27 champagne glasses.

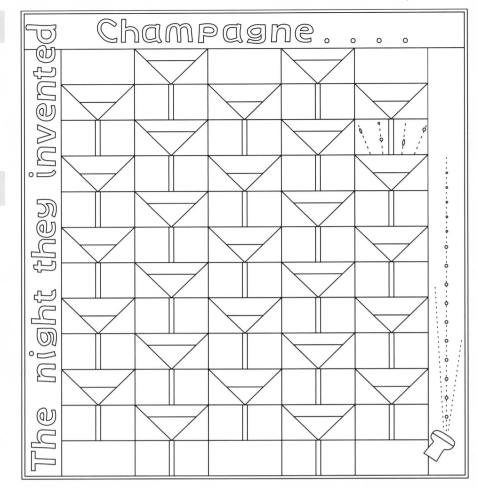

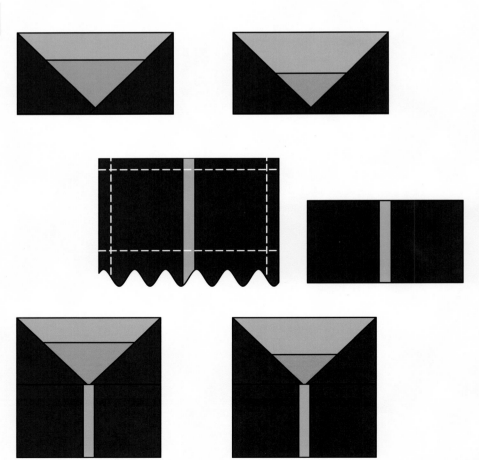

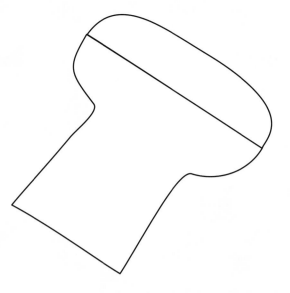

Template for the champagne cork at bottom right of the quilt

2   Making the quilt top

Join glasses in vertical rows – three rows of five glasses and two rows of six glasses. Add a 3½″ × 6½″ rectangle to top and bottom of each five glass row.

Join the vertical rows as shown in the diagram, placing the five glass rows on the centre and on the outside.

3   Borders

Add a 3½″ strip of background fabric to the top and each side of the quilt only.

4   Finishing

Embellish with bias tape lettering or embroidery, plus beads for bubbles. Appliqué a cork to the bottom corner.

Layer and quilt as desired.

Details of the quilt, showing the lettering and the surface decoration that make this such a lively and exciting composition.

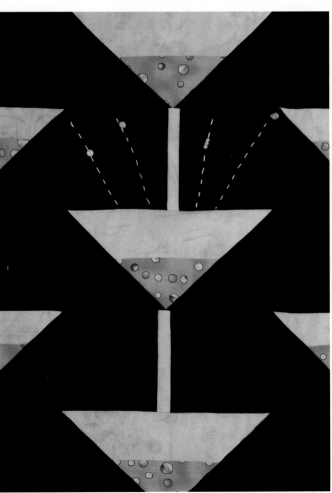

Geese in a bag

Fabric needed

¾ yard from each of two contrasting fabrics.
Craft size medium weight cotton wadding.

Two bag handles.

Cutting

From each of two contrasting fabrics cut:

- Six 2½″ × 4½″ rectangles; twelve 2½″ squares (geese)
- Four 1½″ × 6½″ strips
- Four 6½″ squares
- Two 6¼″ × 18½″ rectangles (lining)
- Two 3″ × 1½″ rectangles (loops)

From medium weight cotton wadding cut four 6½″ × 18½″ rectangles

Instructions

Geese in a bag
*designed and made
by Karin Hellaby*

1 Make 12 flying geese units using the recs and squares technique on page 15. You will have two colourways of six geese. Stitch together in four sets of three geese, two sets in one colour and two sets in the second colour. Press.

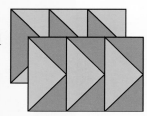

2 Stitch a 1½″ × 6½″ strip to each side of a geese set. Press away from geese.

3 Stitch a 6½″ square to each end. Press away from geese.

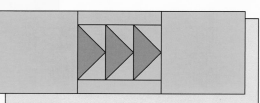

4 Place each completed geese panel on top of a 6½″ × 18½″ rectangle of medium weight cotton wadding. Quilt as desired.

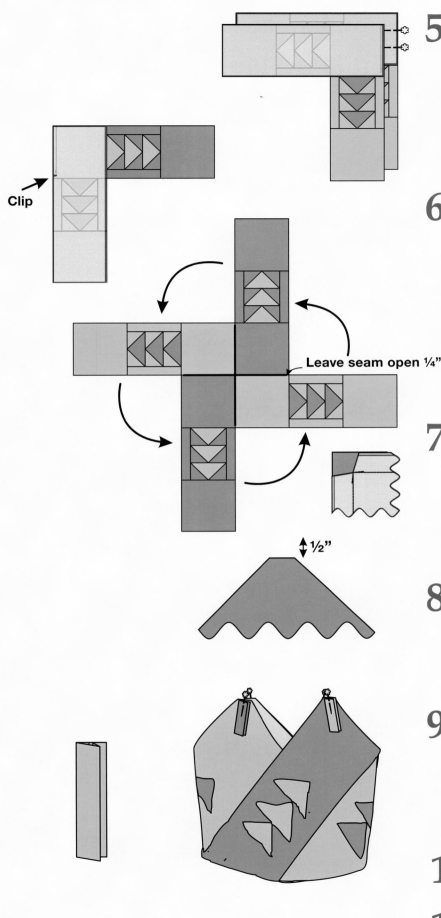

Clip

Leave seam open ¼"

½"

5 Take contrasting pairs of geese panels and position them right sides together with the short side of one piece against the long side of the other. Tip – assemble both sets before sewing because how you do this determines whether your bag swirls to the right or to the left.

6 Stitch pairs of panels together, stopping ¼" from the end. Fasten off. Clip longer edge at the point where stitching stopped so that the long side can be turned on this point. Sew the pairs right sides together starting and stopping ¼" from the ends. You need to get this windmill arrangement.

7 Stitch side seams as shown, finishing ¼" from top end. Fasten off. Press seams open. Blunt top tips by removing ½" from tip. Attach loops made from a 3" × 1½" rectangle which has had its raw edges turned in and stitched.

8 Make lining by stitching together four 6¼" × 18¼" rectangles in the same way as bag outer fabric panels, leaving a gap in one side seam of 6", for turning through.

9 Right sides together, matching and pinning bag top edges, stitch lining to bag. Turn through to right sides, trim the wadding and snip where necessary and finish off side seam lining.

10 Roll and edge stitch bag top edges (optional).

11 Attach handles. Hand stitch the loop on the inside of the bag.

Gift tree

For her *Gift Tree* quilt (42″ × 55″) Theresa Wardlaw placed an appliqué 'gift' behind each of the prairie geese that form the body of the tree. The geese can be untied to flap down and show the hidden appliqué. Variations – hang a small gift or charm behind each goose.

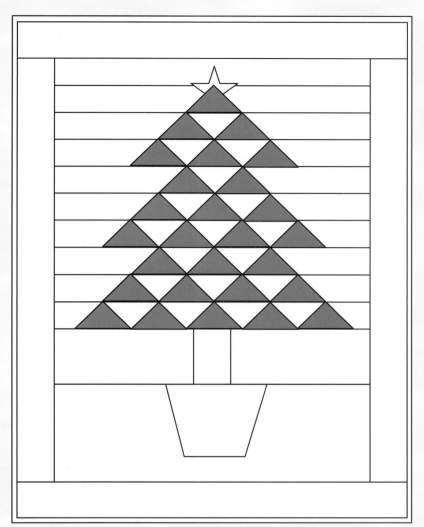

Fabric

Cream background – 2 yards

¼ yard of six different green fabrics

⅛ yard tree bark fabric

Tree pot – 12″ square

Borders – ½ yard

Cutting

- From cream background fabric cut:
  - 10 strips 3½″ × 34½″ (you can add 1 or 2 inches to the length and cut down to final size on all cream fabric strips)
  - 2 pieces 6½″ × 15½″
  - 1 piece 11½″ × 34½″
- Green fabric: cut 5 × 6½″ squares from each of six different fabrics.
- Brown 'bark' fabric: cut one piece 4½″ × 6½″
- Gift fabric: use template to cut pot shape; 12″ square (approx.) to bond and fussy cut.
- Border fabrics: cut 5½″ strips across width of fabric.

Instructions

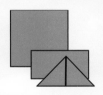

1 Make 30 prairie geese from green squares using method and instructions on page 41. Only 27 geese are needed but you will have three spare geese to help with distributing the different fabrics.

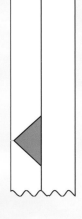

2 Starting at the top of the tree, mark the centre of each goose with a pin. Find the centre of a cream strip and match centres, pinning the goose fold side down. Pin a second strip on top and sew.

3 Press away from the green fabric.

QH Tip

Y ou are sewing through six layers of fabric – make sure you pin firmly to avoid the layers shifting.

Y ou might like to consider using a walking foot on your sewing machine.

4 Lay two more geese on the second strip of background fabric, butt the geese up to each other under the line of the first sewn goose (see diagram). Layer with a third cream strip, pin and sew as before. Continue working down the tree row by row referring to placement diagram.

5 Sew a 6½″ × 15½″ cream rectangle to either side of the brown bark rectangle, giving a unit 6½″ × 34½″. Add this unit over the last row of pinned geese.

6 Sew a large rectangle 11½″ × 34½″ to tree trunk unit and press away from the brown fabric. Centre the appliqué pot shape under the tree trunk and sew using your favourite method.

7 Bond a piece of gift fabric to Steam-a-Seam 2 and cut out the individual motifs. Place two or three behind each goose and bond down.

8 Sew last cream strip onto top row and bond or appliqué a gold star on the top two rows.

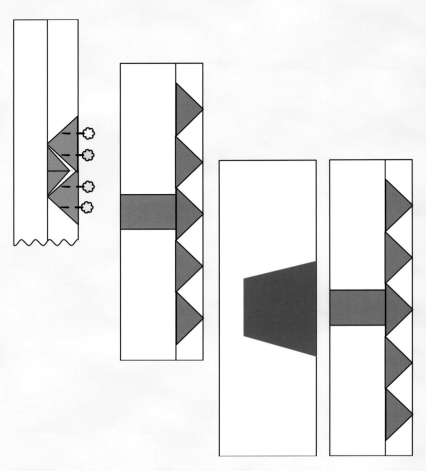

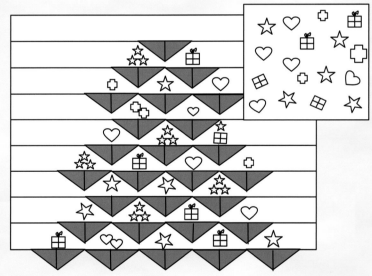

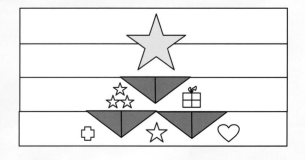

70

9 Square off the edges of the quilt top to a finished size of 34½″ × 47½″.

10 Sew border strips to sides, then top.

11 Layer and quilt in a grid pattern behind geese shapes. The background was quilted with large and small stars to match those on the fabrics. Small stars were quilted in the border. Bind the quilt with a 2½″ folded binding strip.

12 Sew a gold bauble to the background at each point that a goose tip touches. Attach a loop of cord or ribbon to the tip of each goose to wrap around the bauble and hold the goose in position.

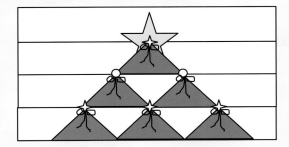

Fold

What if...

...the pockets formed by the folds in the geese are used to hide a treat such as a chocolate coin or small sweet?

Christmas pillow

Cutting

- Centre fabric: cut four 6½″ squares and one 13″ square

- Fabric 1: cut eight 6½″ squares

- Fabric 2: cut eight 6½″ squares

- Fabric 3 and corners: cut four 6½″ squares and four 8½″ squares

- Borders: cut four 3½″ × 22″ strips

- Cushion back: cut two pieces 24″ × 18½″ and 18½″ × 18½″

*18″ square
Christmas pillows
designed and made
by Karin Hellaby*

This pillow always impresses!
Start at the centre and place
geese in layers radiating outwards to
form a star. Experiment with other
fabrics, too – you don't need to limit
this design to Christmas, and it's a
wonderful way to use up scrap fabric.

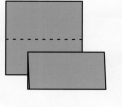

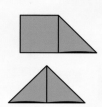

Instructions

1 Using the centre fabric 6½" squares, fold into prairie geese as shown. Fold a square in half, right sides out into a rectangle. Press.

2 Fold sides in towards centre, as shown in diagram, and press.

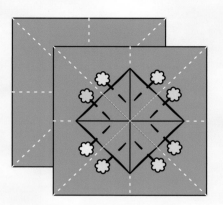

3 Mark lines on the right side of the 13" square as shown. Place the four centre prairie geese in position so that points all meet in the centre. Pin and stitch to fasten the geese down.

QH Tip

Use an invisible thread as the top thread, with coloured thread that matches the 13" square underneath. Stitch in between the centre goose fold from tip to base.

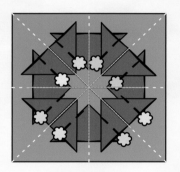

4 Place the eight Fabric 1 prairie geese so that their points are 1¼" away from centre. Centre fold must be placed on the marked foundation line. Pin and stitch between the folds.

5 Place the eight Fabric 2 prairie geese so that the points are 2" away from centre. Again the centre folds must be placed on the marked foundation line. Pin and stitch between folds.

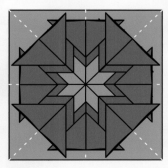

6 Place the four Fabric 3 prairie geese so that they are 3" away from centre and parallel to sides of the foundation square. Centre fold must be placed on the marked foundation line. Pin and stitch between folds.

7 Fold the four 8½" squares as shown and place in corners 3" from centre. Pin and stitch.

8 Stitch borders to each side of the pillow. Sew on each strip, matching the centre of the strip to the centre of the border strip. Sew the border on, starting ¼" in, and finish ¼" from the end. Repeat with the next border.

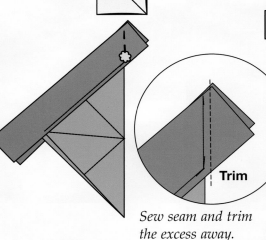

Sew seam and trim the excess away.

Mitre the front diagonally as shown and pin (if necessary check that the mitre lies flat) and sew. Finish your seam at the point where your first seam started. Repeat with the other sides.

Cushion back envelope style

Cut two fabric rectangles 24" × 18½" and 18½" square.

Fold each in half right sides out (this will give you a double layer pillow back).

Position on pillow front so that the rectangles overlap across the centre, smaller underneath. Raw edges at pillow and rectangle sides must match.

Stitch ¼" seam all the way round.

Turn pillow through to right side.

Optional pillow back closure

Three buttonholes can be stitched close to one folded edge on the pillow back and buttons added.

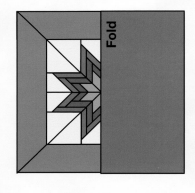

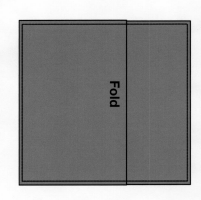

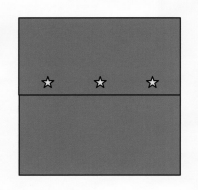

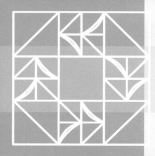

Christmas runners

Runners made by Karin Hellaby and Julia Reed (approximately 17" × 50")

Any festive table will be enhanced by these attractive runners created from three goose blocks set on point and made of coordinating fabrics. Christmas reds, greens and creams produce stunning centrepieces but so also do other interesting colourways.

Fabric (Christmas)

¾ yard main cream colour

Skinny quarter yards of two reds, two greens and one other cream.

75

Cutting

- Side triangles: two 13″ squares in cream.

- Blocks:

  - Corner squares: six 4⅞″ squares in cream; three 4⅞″ squares in red; three 4⅞″ squares in green.

  - Centre square: three 4½″ squares in cream.

- 3D half and half geese: 48 2½″ squares in cream; 24 2½″ squares in red; 24 2½″ squares in green.

Instructions

1 Construct 24 3D red and green half and half geese following instructions on page 22. Take care to produce 12 red-green and 12 green-red geese.

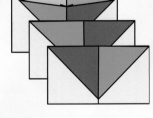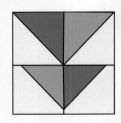

2 Sew pairs of geese together to create 12 squares, four for each of three blocks.

3 Create six red-cream half square triangles from the larger red and cream squares and six green-cream half square triangles from the larger green and cream squares as described on page 22.

4 Assemble the blocks in three rows using the large alternative cream fabric in the centre of the block.

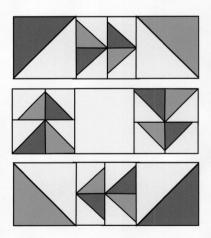

5 Optionally curve the red wings of each split goose.

6 Cut the largest cream squares in two diagonally.

7 Assemble the runner as in the diagram.

8 Layer, quilt and bind.

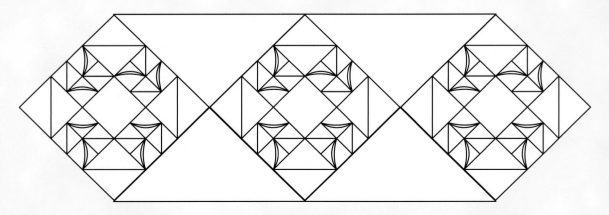

Penguins on ice!

Penguins on ice, *designed and made by Karin Hellaby, machine quilted by Jan Chandler (55" square)*

Sometimes you see a fabric and you just have to have it! The penguin fabric was one of these, and before I knew it this quilt was designed in my head. It took a little longer to sew, but I hope you enjoy making it as much as I did.

Fabric needed

Penguin – 2 yards
Blue Ice – 1 yard
Five colours – ½ yard of each
Light background – 1 yard

Cutting

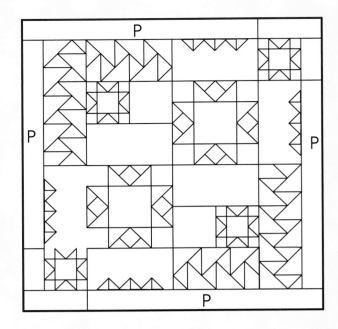

Penguin fabric

- Borders: cut two 4½″ strips across the bolt and then from fabric length cut two 4½″ strips at least 48″ long.
- Fussy cut two 8½″ squares and four 4½″ squares (blocks).

Ice fabric

- Cut three 8½″ strips – cut into six 8½″ × 16½″ rectangles and two 8½″ squares.
- Cut two 4½″ strips – cut into eight 4½″ squares.
- Cut one 2½″ strip – cut into 16 2½″ squares.
- Border: cut two 4½″ × 13″ rectangles, cut two 4½″ × 8½″ rectangles.

Five coloured fabrics

- From each of five fabrics – cut two 6⅝″ squares (for migrating geese).
- From each of four fabrics – cut six 4½″ squares and eight 2½″ squares.

- From fifth fabric (purple) cut eight 4½″ × 8½″ rectangles and four 4½″ squares.

Light background fabric

- Cut two 2½″ strips, cut into 16 2½″ × 4½″ rectangles (small blocks).
- Cut two 4½″ strips, cut into 16 4½″ squares (large blocks).
- Cut four 6¼″ strips, cut into 20 × 6¼″ squares (migrating geese).

Instructions

1 Centre theme squares

Make eight geese using 8″ recs and squares (page 15) with eight purple 4½″ × 8½″ rectangles and 16 × 4½″ squares from the light background. Make the finished geese units into diamond geese (page 20) by adding sixteen 4½″ squares in the four remaining colours fabric. Stitch two finished diamond geese to either side of the two 8½″ penguin squares, press towards centre square. Stitch a 4½″ ice square to each side of remaining four diamond geese units, press towards ice fabric, then sew to top and bottom of each penguin square.

2 Smaller penguin squares (4)

Make sixteen geese using recs and squares instructions on page 15 with 16 2½″ × 4½″ rectangles in light background fabric and eight 2½″ squares from each of the four coloured fabrics. Stitch two finished geese units to either side of the small penguin squares. Press towards centre square.

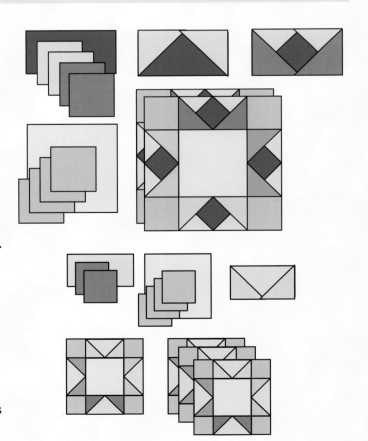

78

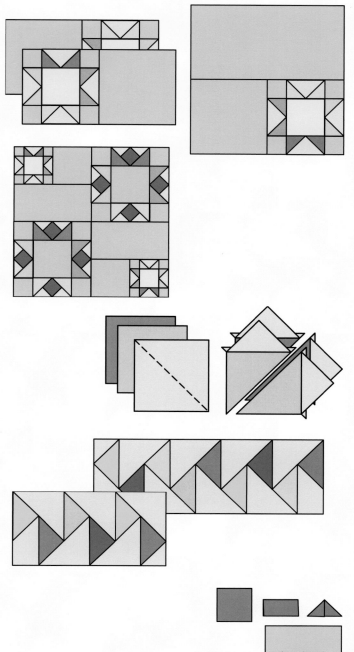

Stitch a 2½" ice square to each side of remaining four diamond geese units, press towards ice fabric and then sew to top and bottom of each penguin square.

3 Assembling central section

Stitch an 8½" square to the **left** side of a small goosed penguin square. Stitch an 8½" square to the **right** side of a small goosed penguin square. Stitch a 8½" × 16½" rectangle to this unit, referring to layout diagram. Press seams towards the ice fabric.

Stitch these units to large goose penguin units. Stitch pairs together to make quilt centre. Press.

4 Migrating geese border

Make thirty migrating geese using 8" finished measurements (instructions on page 36). Stitch two rows of nine migrating geese. Stitch each row to an 8½" × 16½" rectangle. Stitch to quilt sides finishing 3" from end. You will have partially floating border strips.

Sew remaining migrating geese into two rows of six geese. Stitch each row to an 8½" × 16½" background rectangle. Press. Add a small goosed penguin square to one end of nine geese rows. Stitch rows to top and bottom of quilt. Press. Finish off partial seam on side rows.

5 Prairie geese

Use 4½" squares in various colours to make 12 prairie geese (see page 41). Pin and baste in position.

6 Finishing the quilt

Final border

Stitch ice fabric rectangles to border strips. Stitch border strips to quilt. Layer and quilt as desired.

Binding

Cut 4½" strips from each of four coloured fabrics. Stitch together along length. Press seams open.

Cut 2¼" pieces at right angles to seams. Stitch together to make a binding length.

Below: Ice floe quilting!

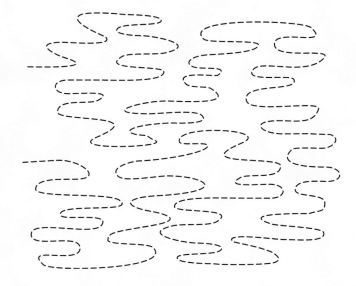

Using the same instructions as *Penguins on ice*, Sheila has made a quilt with a farm theme.

Choose any fabric where you want to show off a large design: butterflies, fish, flowers, cats, dogs, or any other subject that particularly appeals to you!

In laying out your design you may find it useful to refer to the fussy cutting and fussy appliqué on page 8.

Down on the Farm
by Sheila Marr (55" square)

Flannel posies

Flannel makes up into a lovely, cuddly quilt that can also be backed up with polyester fleece. This lap size quilt would make a delightful gift. It's a great mix of patchwork piecing and appliqué that gives an attractive scrapbook effect.

Top of page: Flannel Posies *by Karin Hellaby (43" square)*

Left: Pastel Posies *by Muriel Cox (43" square)*

81

Fabric needed

Fabric needed for centre flower squares: 26 obese eighth yards in light and dark fabrics.

Cutting instructions

- Centre flower blocks:

  - From each of the 8 light and 8 dark obese eighths cut 2″ × 20″ strip, one 6½″ square and one 5″ square.

  - From 2″ strips cut one 6½″ length and two 5″ lengths.

  - From each of **eight remaining** eighths (4 light and 4 dark) cut two 2″ strips, along the length.

  - From each of these strips cut one 6½″ length and two 5″ lengths.

- The two remaining eighths will be used in the border.

Instructions

1 Stitching a frame around each square

Stitch dark 2″ × 6½″ lengths to opposite sides of light 6½″ squares. Press seam away from centre square.

Stitch light 2″ × 6½″ lengths to opposite sides of dark 6½″ squares. Press seam away from centre square.

Stitch 5″ lengths in pairs (light to another light, dark to another dark) along short sides to make 9½″ lengths. Stitch 16 dark pairs and 16 light pairs. Press seam to darkest side.

Stitch light pairs to opposite sides of dark squares, stitch dark pairs to opposite sides of light squares. Each centre square should now be surrounded by a frame. Press away from centre square. Finished size of square will be 9½″.

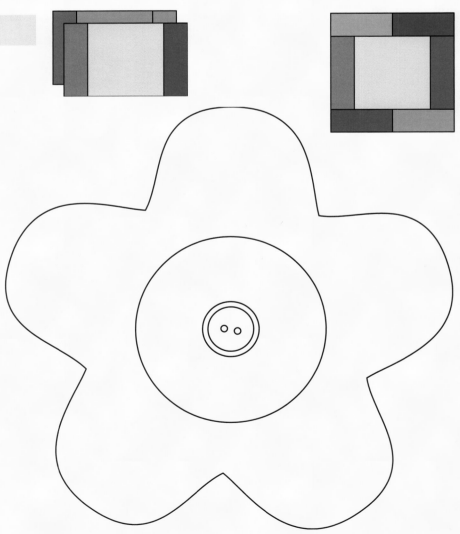

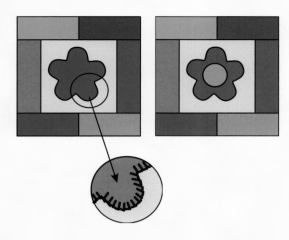

2 Appliqué

Use the 5″ square to cut out flowers using the template on the previous page. Sew a flower onto the centre square, use a light flower inside a dark square and a dark flower inside a light square.

The appliqué method used on this quilt involved bonding the flower using a light Steam-a-Seam 2 and then machine blanket stitch around the raw edges.

The flower centre circle is cut from remains of the 2″ strips and appliquéd in the same way.

Again, light centres were placed on dark flowers and vice versa.

3 Block layout

Arrange alternate dark and light squares (see photograph on page 81), with four squares across and four squares down to make a 16 square quilt top.

Twist squares around so that adjoining frames do not need matching seams i.e. a short side of one block is matched to a paired side of the adjoining block.

Stitch blocks together in horizontal rows.

Press, and stitch rows together to make the quilt top.

4 Border

From remaining dark fabrics cut 4½″ wide strips, varied lengths are fine!

5 Flying Geese

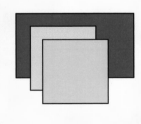

Make 20 Flying Geese using the instructions on page 34.

Stitch five geese together. Repeat with remaining flying geese to make four geese strips.

Stitch dark 4½″ wide dark strips to base of geese strips to make four sides of border approximately 50″ in length.

Stitch to sides of quilt using the photograph as a guide.

Layer, quilt and bind.

I used a polyester fleece for backing and no wadding.

Buttons were sewn into the centre of each flower to tie the fleece to the quilt top.

Quilt plans

These simple quilt plans can be used by the more experienced patchworker. It is left to you to choose the technique and size of geese you wish to make.

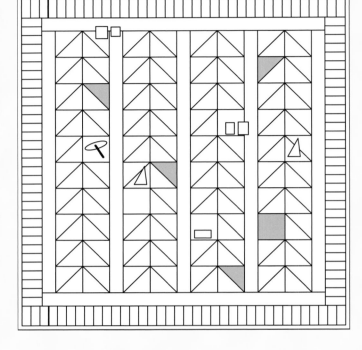

Above: Sea and Sand *by Karin Hellaby* (36" × 38")

Below: Tropical Flocks *by Karin Hellaby* (55" × 64")

Above: Lilac Wine *by Liz Powell*
(55″ × 66″)

Below: Geese in the Forest *by Anne Smith*
(48″ × 60″)

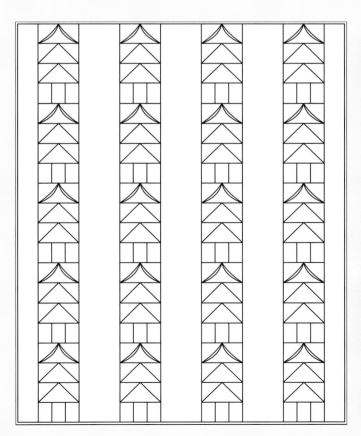

85

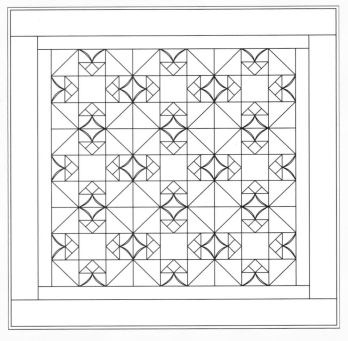

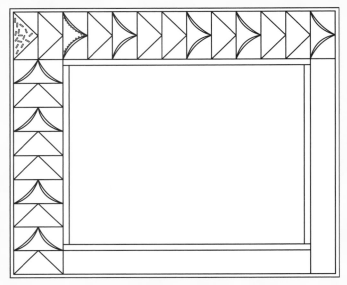

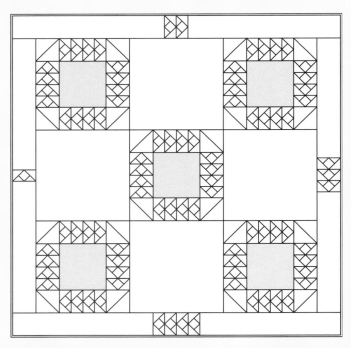

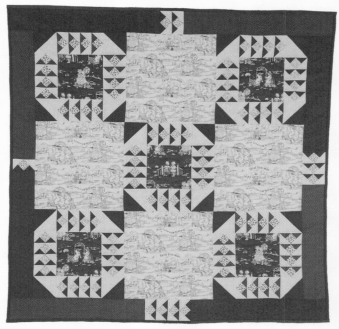

Opposite page, from top:

Raspberry Ripple *by Heather Langdon (49" square)*

Winter Wonderland *by Karin Hellaby, beading by Debs Gardiner (22" × 26")*

Best Friends *by Dena Daniels, designed by Karin Hellaby (56" square)*

Angel serenade by Julia Reed, from an original doodle by Karin Hellaby (46" square). To use the template on the left, make a photocopy of it at 200%.

The geese that flew away!

There are literally hundreds of quilt blocks featuring geese designs. We have picked some of our favourites for you to play with...!

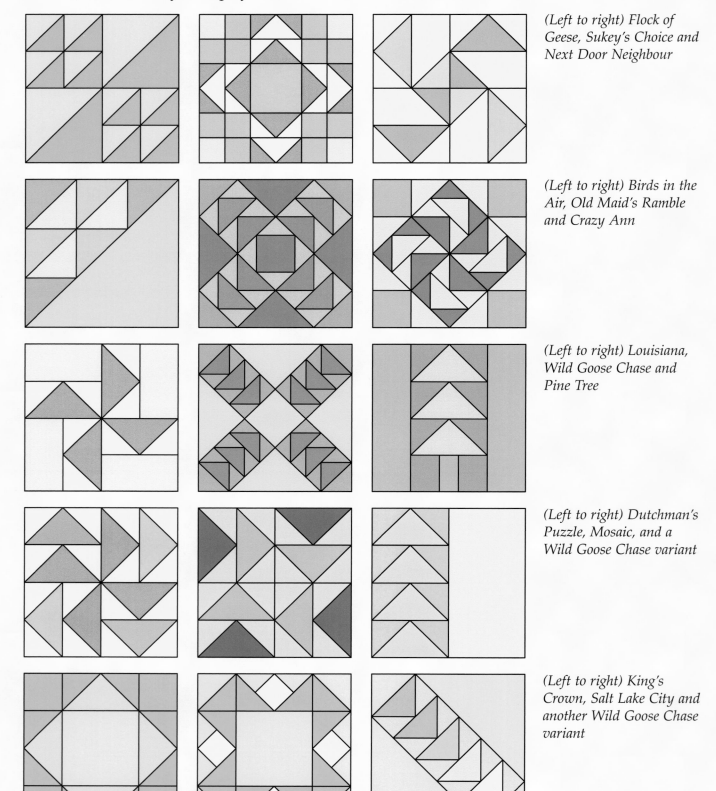

(Left to right) Flock of Geese, Sukey's Choice and Next Door Neighbour

(Left to right) Birds in the Air, Old Maid's Ramble and Crazy Ann

(Left to right) Louisiana, Wild Goose Chase and Pine Tree

(Left to right) Dutchman's Puzzle, Mosaic, and a Wild Goose Chase variant

(Left to right) King's Crown, Salt Lake City and another Wild Goose Chase variant

Quilt designs created from the blocks and techniques described in this book, including the quilt the graphic artist would have made if her time hadn't flown away!

Quilt gallery

With so many beautiful quilts to choose from, it was inevitable that not every quilt could feature in the projects, or in the techniques section. So here are some of the quilts that got away – with my very grateful thanks to the people who made them..

Indian summer *by Val Derks (66" square); notice the lovely little goose at bottom right (see close up, right).*

Top (left and right):
Crazy Geese by
Lin Patterson
(both 21″ × 35″)

Right:
Wait for Georgia
by Julia Reed
(35″ × 29″).
Georgia is a crazy
patchwork goose with yarn
couched round her body to
give a feathery look.

91

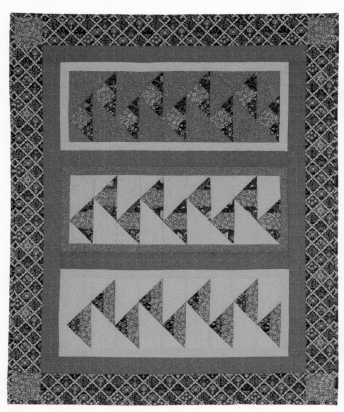

Above: Geese sampler *by Julia Reed (28″ × 34″)*

Above: Flying North, looking East
by Marion Barnes (53″ × 55″)

Below: Poppy Power *by Erica Ransom of
North Carolina (39″ × 59)″ and quilted
by Judy Whitehead*

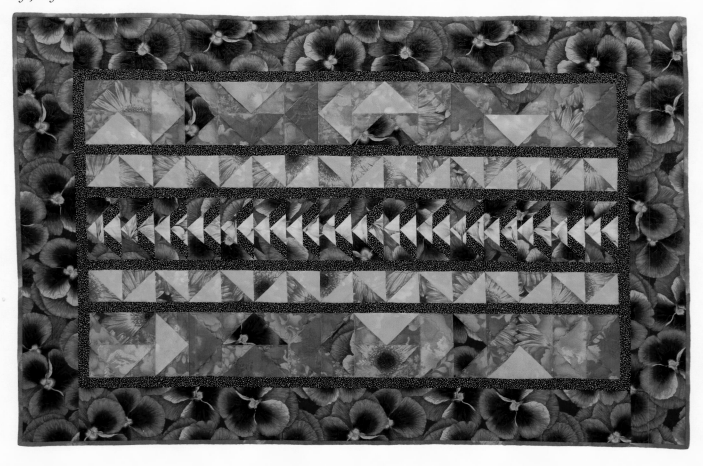

92

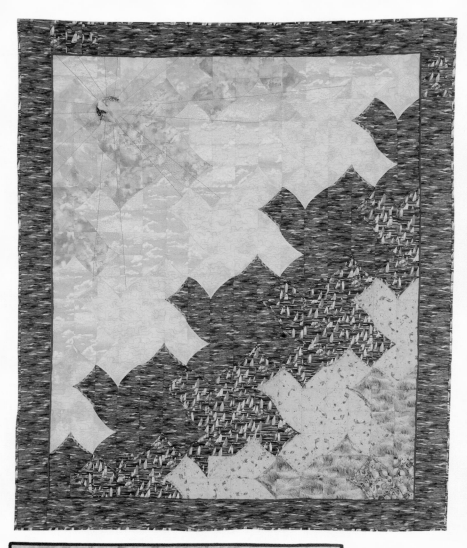

Above: Geese on the River (54″ × 66″) *by* Carole Redman

Left: Sunflowers on Parade *by Grace Howes, North Carolina 39″ × 52″, quilted by Judy Whitehead*

Right: An assortment of bags made by Karin Hellaby, Ann Whatling and Julia Reed

93

Addresses

For all your sewing needs

Quilters Haven
68 High Street, Wickham Market
Suffolk IP13 0QU, UK

Tel: +44 (0)1728 746275
Fax: +44 (0)1728 746314

Shop opening hours: 9 am – 5 pm,
Monday to Saturday
(Some evening and Sunday openings
dependent on class schedules)

Fully secure on-line shop on:
www.quilters-haven.co.uk

E-mail: quilters.haven@btinternet.com

Design and layout

Creative Computing
Rosemary Muntus and Allan Scott
Old Mill House, The Causeway,
Hitcham, Suffolk IP7 7NF, UK

Tel: +44 (0)1449 741747

E-mail: design@thecraftycomputer.com
Web: www.thecraftycomputer.com

Distribution outside the UK

Quilters' Resource Inc.
PO Box 148850
Chicago
Illinois 60614
USA

Tel: 773-278-5695
Fax: 773-278-1348

Web: www.quiltersresource.com

About the author

Karin Hellaby was born in the north-east of England of Norwegian parents: her first language was Norwegian. She studied for a Home Economics teaching degree from the University of Wales. She now lives in Suffolk, UK, and is the single parent of three wonderful sons. Karin started teaching quiltmaking around her kitchen table when pregnant with her third son, Alexander, who is now 15 years old. Quilters Haven opened in 1993 as a teaching centre, with a shop alongside to supply the students, a unique concept in England at that time. It moved to its 16th-century timber-framed building in 1996. The attractive shop and teaching room brings in quiltmakers and teachers from all over the world. In 1998 Karin, with the help of her son Ross (then aged 15), won the Kile Scholarship – International Retailer of the Year. The next step was to write a book. That was **Sew a Row Quilts!** Later she published a companion pattern book, **Sew a Row Projects**.

As a shop owner and teacher, Karin is in a position where she can sometimes see when a new book is needed. **Magic Pillows, Hidden Quilts** was written for such a gap. She loves travelling and has enjoyed teaching at the International quilt markets and festivals in the USA and Europe.